ALAN TURING
THE ENIGMA MAN

ALAN TURING
THE ENIGMA MAN

NIGEL CAWTHORNE

ARCTURUS

ARCTURUS

This edition published in 2014 by
Arcturus Publishing Limited
26/27 Bickels Yard, 151–153 Bermondsey Street,
London SE1 3HA

ISBN: 978-1-78404-535-7
AD004448UK

Printed in the UK

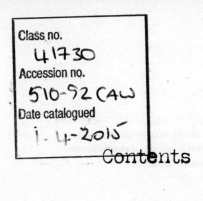

Contents

E97. 9 B. A. A. 1 A. B. O. A B 5 C 3
82 8. 707F25 A 7 9 A2 DD F. 1 1A D9C0 A
5A446 04B27A1C E 3BCDE 81E89B. 4549BCDC
.B827. 9B8DBA89BA677D45FF8DF75A34AD
7E0342ADC9672D8EE8F46FF90E62F2C061DC
8AB90AA91DCE19EA87D45B827496 2C6 C873 C8
BA3087D38CBAB2B446FF0342AD9 9 AA 1E8BA
90472D8ADCCB3087D38AB245A6BA1B2B449ADA

INTRODUCTION

· · · · · · · · · · · · · · ·

Breakthrough at
Bletchley Park

342ADC1F25B430D9C00A6D8DF75A34F4129672D8EE
A91DC06E97BEA6A8E13F2E62E2C061ADCE19EA8
7D38C89EA8707F25BADAC62C6EC8789FCBAB2B
6BA1B2B4490AA91D4789C9BAA1E3F021DADCC
4F4161ADCCB3087D38AB27A8EE6137A1C389FCE03
2BEB010FF7BA8C878906E97BCDEA8E3F0290
CA2 0DF90 472 1E3 F89EA87D45FF38FD26D982
A1 6E 349 C C6 3 A1B2B446FF907256E80B10
8AB27A1C6EB33BCAB850CC89EA87D45FF7BA4AA0
8DBA89BA675B430D9C0A1B2B446FF9047238
34AA1C6B4. 0D9. 003F2E6D248F6D 8C89EE85EC
7A B7B A6A 1 AC 2 FB 0 BA1B 850C
A. 2 E. 7 7 2 . 78 C 2 F . 6 A D9

In 1940, Britain's Second World War codebreaking operation at Bletchley Park, Buckinghamshire, could claim some success in cracking the 'Red' code used by the German air force. Using a machine called a bombe, perfected by Alan Turing, Hut 6 could decode messages sent by the Luftwaffe, allowing the Royal Air Force to shoot German aircraft out of the skies. As a result, Adolf Hitler had to cancel his plans to mount a seaborne invasion of Britain, known as Operation Sealion, which would eventually be abandoned completely.

But Britain was still in dire peril. The Battle of the Atlantic was now in full swing. German U-boats, hunting in 'wolf packs', were sinking merchant shipping carrying the food, fuel, munitions and raw material on which Britain depended at such a rate that the British faced being starved into surrender. The submarines were being directed by messages written in a complicated German navy code generated by now-upgraded naval Enigma machines. These resembled typewriters and were battery-powered and portable.

Their operation was simple enough. When a letter key was pressed another letter lit up on the lamp board above. However, the connection between the keys and the lamp board passed through a series of rotors which moved with every keystroke, so that if the same key was pressed repeatedly a different letter would light up each time. Naval Enigma machines also had a plugboard where other connections were set up, further scrambling the code. Once the message was encoded, it was transmitted by Morse code. If the recipient had an Enigma machine set up in exactly the same way, the message could then be decoded simply by typing in the letters received and writing down those that appeared on the lamp board. Given the millions of possible combinations of rotors and plugboard connections, the Germans thought that the Enigma code was unbreakable. They had not counted on Alan Turing.

The brilliant young mathematician arrived at Bletchley Park at

Turing at around the time he began working at Bletchley Park in September 1939

the beginning of the war and quickly designed the bombe, which rapidly ran through all the possible ways in which the Enigma machine could have been set up, but the ten listening posts that intercepted German Morse transmissions for Bletchley Park were producing so much material that it was impossible to handle it all. And when the Germans' code machines were upgraded, the decoding process took so long that it was too late to take action on the intelligence produced.

The British got lucky when some of the documentation that accompanied the German navy Enigma machines was captured. And then Turing worked out a way to narrow down the number of possible settings that could have been used to produce any coded message. This used 'cribs' – known or guessed stock phrases. One of the minor weaknesses of the Enigma machine was that no letter would be encoded as itself – if you pressed the 'A' any other letter apart from 'A' would light up.

German operators would transmit stock phrases. Weather ships routinely sent 'weather for the night' – rendered without spaces as 'WETTERFUERDIENACHT' – or 'situation eastern Channel' – 'ZUSTANDOSTWAERTIGER-KANAL'. If such a phrase was run alongside a coded message it was sometimes possible to find a place where no letters matched, giving a possible translation for that part of the message and narrowing the number of possible settings used at the beginning of the message.

There were plenty of common phrases like 'nothing special to report' and 'Heil Hitler' or 'Führer' often appeared at the beginning or end of messages. Better still, from a captured German wireless operation it was discovered that if transmission had been broken off for whatever reason it resumed with 'FORT' – an abbreviation for *Fortsetzung* or 'continuation'. This was followed by a number identifying the previous message, usually the time it had been sent. This would be spelled out in full, so 2300 would be 'ZWEIDREINULNUL'. The Germans also transmitted map references. Turing studied letter sequencing in the German language as well. For example, 'eins' and 'sch' are common sequences of letters in German, but 'jgt' is not common, if it exists at all.

To exploit these weaknesses, Turing, who was in charge of Hut 8, tasked with breaking the German navy code, came up with a system he called Banburism. He had a workshop in Banbury, Oxfordshire, which produced special punched paper strips. When one section of text was run over another, it was possible to spot matches. These methods reduced the millions of possible settings of the Enigma machine down to hundreds of thousands, which Turing's bombe could just about handle.

German soldiers communicate using an Enigma encoding machine, c.1942

He then used Bayesian statistics, first developed by 18th-century British mathematician Thomas Bayes, to work out the most probable initial settings, so that these could be tested first instead of churning through tens of thousands.

In April 1941, the team at Bletchley Park set about trying to decode messages as they came in. By June they were cracking them within a few hours of their interception. Prime Minister Winston Churchill's war planners had predicted that Britain would tip into starvation in that very month. But using 'Ultra' – as intelligence from the decryption of enemy ciphers was known – British shipping was able to evade the wolf packs so successfully that for twenty-three consecutive days U-boats in the North Atlantic made not a single sighting of a convoy.

The following month Turing and his colleagues were summoned to Whitehall to be thanked officially. They received a £200 bonus, the equivalent of £6,000 in today's money, and Churchill paid a visit to Bletchley Park. He was taken to Hut 8 to meet Turing, who was 'very nervous'.

Churchill described the codebreakers there as 'the geese that lay the golden eggs – and never cackle'.

As the U-boats continued to scour the North Atlantic fruitlessly, there were fears that the Germans might realize that their codes had been broken, so information was leaked that the British had developed a new long-range radar that could detect submarines hundreds of miles away, even when they were under water. This was unnecessary, because in the paranoid Nazi regime it was assumed that some spy was passing details of the U-boat movements to the British.

The battle had been won, but the war continued. Intercepted messages were coming in at such a rate that the cryptanalysts at Bletchley Park were overwhelmed. In October 1941, Turing and others wrote to Churchill saying:

'Dear Prime Minister,
Some weeks ago you paid us the honour of a visit, and we believe that you regard our work as important. You will have seen that . . . we have been well supplied with the "bombes" for the breaking of the German Enigma codes. We think,

The sinking of the Empire Mica, *a British tanker, after a torpedo attack by the German submarine U-67 on 29 June 1942*

however, that you ought to know that this work is being held up, and in some cases is not being done at all, principally because we cannot get sufficient staff to deal with it. Our reason for writing to you direct is that for months we have done everything that we possibly can through the normal channels, and we despair of any early improvement without your intervention.'

Churchill immediately responded with a memo which read:

> 'Action this Day
> Make sure they have all they want on extreme priority and report to me that this has been done.'

Churchill later wrote: 'The only thing that ever frightened me during the war was the U-Boat peril.'

With the wolf packs defeated in the North Atlantic and the United States joining the war on the Allies' side in December 1941, not only was Britain saved from starvation, but it was possible to stockpile men and munitions in the British Isles ready for the invasion of Normandy in 1944. And the man responsible for that was Alan Turing.

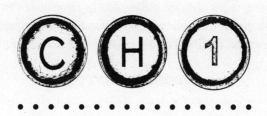

CH 1

Birth of a Genius

Alan Turing was a child of the Empire. His father Julius Mathison Turing was an assistant administrator and magistrate in the Madras province of British India. His mother, Sara, was the daughter of the chief engineer of the Madras Railway. Born in Madras and brought up in Ireland, she attended lectures at the Sorbonne in Paris before meeting Julius, a history graduate of Corpus Christi College, Oxford, on a cruise ship in the Orient. When they reached Japan, he asked her out. They married a few months later in Dublin in 1907. The following year their first son, John, was born in her parents' house at the hill station of Coonoor.

TROUBLED TIMES

In 1912, Sara was pregnant again. By then political unrest had made India a dangerous place for British administrators. The viceroy, Lord Charles Hardinge, was the target of a number of assassination attempts by militant Indian nationalists and that year he was wounded by a bomb during his state entry into Delhi.

Julius took leave and the family travelled back to England. They rented a house in Maida Vale, north London, and their second son was born in Warrington Lodge, a nursing home in Little Venice, on 23 June 1912. He was christened Alan Mathison at St Saviour's Church in Warrington Avenue two weeks later.

When Alan was nine months old, his father returned to India. Six months later, his mother Sara followed. She had intended to take Alan with her, but the toddler was suffering from rickets. So the two boys were left in the charge of Colonel and Mrs Ward in Hastings. Once the First World War had got under way, the colonel encouraged the boys to play with toy guns, cannons and battleships, but they rebelled.

In 1915, their mother risked the journey through submarine-infested waters to pay a visit. She found Alan disturbed. Writing home to her husband, she said:

'Alan will in a moment cry with rage and attempt to hold his breath, and in the next moment he will laugh at his tears, saying, "Look at my big tears," squeeze his eyes and say, "Ah" with his mouth wide open trying to squeeze out more tears for fun.'

However, he was a pretty, outgoing and engaging boy, quite free of the shyness that would afflict him later at public school. His mother said: 'I was not alone in my opinion when I wrote that he was "a very clever child, I should say, with a wonderful memory for new words".'

After three months in her care, his mother wrote: 'Alan has improved greatly. He has many charming traits. He misses nothing.' He had a lively mind and that summer, she noted, he made his first attempt at experimenting.

'One of the wooden sailors in his toy boat got broken,' she recalled. 'He planted the arms and legs in the garden, confident that they would grow into toy sailors.'

When his mother returned to India that autumn, she asked Alan to be a good boy while she was away. He said: 'Yes, but sometimes I forget.' Even John, something of a rebel himself, said: 'Alan was quite a nuisance.'

In March 1916, Julius and Sara braved the U-boats again, wearing life-belts all the way from Suez to Southampton. They took a holiday in Scotland before Julius returned to India. Given the U-boat menace, it was decided that Sara should stay in England with the boys. By then John was at prep school, so Alan lived with his mother in rooms in St Leonards-on-Sea.

EARLY SIGNS OF BRILLIANCE

From an early age, Alan was interested in figures. Even before he could read he would study the serial numbers on the lampposts around Hastings. At first, he did not know whether to read the numbers from right to left or vice versa. However, he noticed a red spot on his left thumb which he called the 'knowing spot'. When he came across a number he would pull back his glove and look for the spot, then he would know which way to read the figures.

It was clear that he had an unusual mind. At five, he announced that rhubarb made his teeth feel as if the white had come off. Later, when his father was back in England again, he told young Alan off for having the tongues of his boots twisted. 'Those tongues should be as flat as a pancake,' said Julius.

'Pancakes are usually rolled up,' Alan shot back.

He also made up words. 'Quockling' was his word for the noise made by seagulls fighting over food, a 'greasicle' was the rivulet of wax down the side of a candle when it is caught in a draught and 'squaddy' was Alan's word for being squat and square.

However, Alan lagged behind when being taught to read. Then he came across a book called *Reading Without Tears* and taught himself to read in three weeks. This self-reliance when it came to problem solving would become a trademark.

In 1918, he went to St Michael's Primary School where he began to learn Latin. When he left at the age of nine, the headmistress there said: 'I have had clever boys and hard-working boys, but Alan is a genius.'

Outside school, Alan was precocious. He pounded up dock leaves to make a cure for nettle stings, precisely recording the formula, and began compiling what he called an 'encyclopaedio'. Waking early he would write down sundry facts such as the width of England. Geography held a special appeal and he asked for an atlas for his birthday. Later, when Alan arrived at his prep school, Hazelhurst, he beat older brother John in a school-wide geography test.

Alan's other passion was reading nature-study books and at the age of eight he began writing a book called *About a Microscope*. That summer, the family took a holiday in Scotland where Alan carefully observed the flight of bees and tracked them to their nest to get their honey. In the evenings Sara read *Pilgrim's Progress* to the two boys, but when she decided to skip some of the heavier theological discussion Alan was indignant. Shouting 'You spoilt the whole thing', he dashed from the room and stamped up and down in a huff.

That autumn Julius and Sara returned to India once more. Alan wrote to them regularly, talking of his newest concoctions including the recipe for his 'gobletoe drink', which contained grass roots, radish leaves and nettles. He then wrote an advertisement for Dunlop in the hope that they would send him free tyres for his bicycle. But Mrs Ward wrote to his parents, complaining of Alan's continued stubbornness and disobedience. He rode round and round the lawn on his bicycle and refused to come in, saying: 'I can't get off until I fall off.'

When his mother returned to England in 1921, she found Alan had changed. Formerly outgoing, he was now withdrawn and dreamy. She took him out of school and taught him at home for a term. They spent the summer in Brittany. In London that autumn, he spent his time collecting bits of metal from the gutters with a magnet and he was full of questions. At nine, his mother recalled, he asked: 'What makes the oxygen fit so tightly to the hydrogen to make water?' She had no answer.

After a skiing holiday in Switzerland, Alan began at Hazelhurst where he spent his spare time making paper boats and, to start with, getting into fights. He was soon unpopular at school. Poor at games, he preferred to play chess – though few would play with him – and he spent hours working out complex chess problems on his own. Later in life he became an accomplished runner and said he got his start at school, fleeing from the ball. Teachers considered him both lazy and insolent. He complained that his algebra teacher 'gave a quite false impression of what is meant by x'.

That summer, while holidaying with his family in the Highlands, he went climbing and after hearing a lecture on Everest expressed an interest in joining the next expedition to the as yet unconquered peak. In the evenings, the family dined in the garden and competed to see who could spit gooseberry skins the farthest. Alan won by applying scientific methods. He inflated his skins so they would be more aerodynamic.

At school, he was always building gadgets, including a far from successful fountain pen, and the library records show that he never borrowed fiction. In the holidays, he cycled out to the nearby woods where he experimented, once returning covered in soot and with his eyelashes singed after firing clay pipes he had made. There were experiments with baking soda and muddy jam jars in the coal cellar. Archdeacon Rollo Meyer and his wife, who looked after the boys in the school holidays, wrote to their parents complaining that Alan was always doing dangerous things.

In 1922, he came across the American book *Natural Wonders Every Child Should Know* by E.T. Brewster which, he told his mother later, opened his eyes to science – particularly biology, which became a lifelong interest – and after a holiday in Rouen he began writing to his parents in halting French. Climbing in Wales, he drew maps of the places he had visited. He also took an interest in family trees. Then the gift of a chemistry set afforded new opportunities for experimenting. In the basement, he extracted iodine from seaweed. But his mother fretted, telling a friend: 'I am sure that he will blow up himself and the house one day.'

A schoolmaster gave him private tutoring. He also tutored himself using the form's encyclopaedia. At the age of twelve-and-a-half, he wrote home: 'I always seem to want to make things from the thing that is the commonest in nature and with the least of waste energy.'

PROBLEM PUPIL

In 1924, his father retired, but to avoid heavy taxation on his pension he did not return to England. He and Sara settled in France. By then, though, Alan was used to his parents being some way away. He even took himself to school by taxi, tipping the porter and the driver.

His clear aptitude for science and mathematics did not stand him in good stead in a school that specialized in teaching Latin,

Greek, literature and the classics in preparation for public school. Turing's spelling and grammar were poor – and remained so throughout his life. Nevertheless, he passed his Common Entrance examination and seemed to be destined to follow his brother to Marlborough College. But John warned: 'For God's sake don't send him here. It will crush the life out of him.'

Instead Alan was sent to Sherborne, a 300-year-old public school in Dorset where the husband of one of his mother's friends was science master. Travelling to school from his parents' new home in France, Turing took the ferry from St Malo to Southampton. But when he arrived back in England, it was the first day of the 1926 General Strike and no buses or trains were running. His only option was to cycle the sixty miles to Sherborne, stopping for the night in a hotel on the way and keeping detailed accounts to justify the outlay to his father.

Alan Turing did not excel at his new school. Even his mathematics was 'not very good'. His report said: 'He spends a great deal of time in investigations in advanced mathematics to the neglect of his elementary work.' In his science lessons, which occupied just two hours a week in the classical curriculum, 'his knowledge is scrappy', while his housemaster complained that he was 'trying to build a roof before he has laid the foundations'. However, knowing Alan's aversion to games, his father had requested that Alan substitute golf for cricket. This gave him the opportunity to walk around thinking out problems. As a result he won the school's Plumptre Prize for mathematics. His maths teacher, Mr Randolph, declared him to be a 'genius' after being shown an algebraic exposition. Randolph at first thought Turing must have copied it from a book, but he had worked it out from first principles. But this counted for little at a school that valued the humanities and classics. Generally, his work was so poorly presented that it was thought he ought to be sent down. As his headmaster remarked: 'It is only the shallowest of minds that can suppose . . . scientific discovery brings us appreciably nearer the solution of the

Pupils in a science class at Sherborne School

riddles of the universe.' He considered Turing 'anti-social' and said that he was 'the kind of boy who is bound to be a problem in any kind of school', though the headmaster did concede that Turing had 'special gifts'.

As a boy, Turing was also scruffy and unkempt. This was a particular problem when it came to the Officer Training Corps parade on Fridays. His failure to bond with other boys, and his general 'slackness' in gym, meant that he was considered a 'drip' and was teased for his shyness, his high-pitched voice and his hesitant delivery that almost amounted to a stammer. A classmate said that Turing was 'an example of how a sensitive and inoffensive boy . . . can have his life made hell at public school'.

What annoyed his teachers the most was his ability to pay no attention to them during lessons and then cram at the last minute and score high marks in the final exam. As it was, most of his work in his new obsession, mathematics, was done outside the classroom.

Turing's greatest *bête noire* was his English and Latin teacher A.H.

Trelawney Ross, who believed that Germany had lost the First World War because it thought 'science and materialism were stronger than religious thought and observance'.

'As democracy advances, manners and morals recede,' he said. Scientific subjects were 'low cunning' and when Turing was around he would sniff and say: 'This room smells of mathematics. Go out and fetch a disinfectant spray.'

Turing simply ignored Ross and when the teacher caught him doing algebra during a study period set aside for religious instruction he failed Turing in both taught subjects. Nevertheless, Ross conceded: 'I like him personally.' And, despite Turing's slovenliness, his house-master remarked that he had a 'saving sense of humour'.

As well as being a fount of odd scientific facts, the young Turing made a joke of his own inadequacies in a way that most found endearing. Nevertheless, Turing did not make life easy for himself at school and did not go out of his way to make friends.

At fifteen, Turing wrote a précis of Albert Einstein's *Relativitäts-theorie* (Theory of Relativity), recently published in English, to explain the principles to his mother. For Turing Einstein's work was intoxicating. It overthrew the axioms of Euclid and Newton which until then had been the bedrock of mathematics and science. Turing's brother John remarked:

'You could take a safe bet that if you ventured on some self-evident proposition, as for example that the earth was round, Alan would produce a great deal of incontrovertible evidence to prove that it was almost certainly flat, ovular, or much the same shape as a Siamese cat which had been boiled for fifteen minutes at a temperature of one thousand degrees centigrade.'

FIRST CLOSE FRIENDSHIP

Sherborne had been the setting for old boy Alec Waugh's controversial semi-autobiographical novel *The Loom of Youth*, published in 1917, which openly mentioned homosexual relations between boys. And at some point in Turing's first two years there, he began to discover that he, too, was attracted to his own sex. *The Loom of Youth* was, of course, a banned book at the school and the masters tried to deal with the problem through cold showers and preventing boys studying together without a teacher being present. Turing tried to cope with his growing desires by going on long runs.

His affections became fixed on fellow pupil Christopher Morcom, who became his one school friend. He was a year older than Alan and an outstanding student. They shared an interest in science and mathematics.

Their relationship was innocent enough. Turing wrote that Morcom had some very definite ideas of right and wrong and avoided 'dirty talk', though he was not 'in any way silly or priggish'. Turing and Morcom spent time creating and deciphering codes. They particularly liked codes that used a template – a carefully cut pattern that, when placed over a specific page in a specific book, revealed a secret message. Among youngsters, code making and breaking was all the rage. Codes and ciphers were used by the heroes of comic books and by the 1930s manufacturers of breakfast cereal were promoting their products with 'decoder rings' and other codebreaking devices.

Morcom was an accomplished pianist and introduced Turing to classical music. He also helped Turing improve his social skills and smarten up his appearance and his handwriting. As a result Turing's work improved and he was not picked on so much by the other boys, even attracting some admiration for his long-distance running. In the school's inter-house races, he could beat all-comers.

As Turing began, finally, to fit in at school, his parents' worries were quelled and at home they enjoyed his obvious talents.

'We regarded Alan as the family encyclopaedia,' his mother wrote. 'He seemed to have the answers to all our scientific queries.'

Turing now relished the competition with Morcom in their scientific work.

'Chris's work was always better than mine,' he said. 'He was very thorough. He was certainly very clever but he never neglected details, and for instance very seldom made arithmetical slips. He had a great power in practical work of finding out just what was the best way of doing anything.'

To impress his friend, Turing calculated the value of π to thirty-six decimal places. Teachers described him as 'brilliant', saying that he thought rapidly. But he found schoolwork dull compared to relativity and his grades were low compared with Morcom's.

Morcom also involved Turing in laddish pranks. They dropped stones from a railway bridge down the funnels of passing trains. One bounced off and hit the stoker, nearly getting them into serious trouble. They sent gas-filled balloons across the field to Sherborne Girls' School. And, with another boy, they wrote a sketch ragging a science master, which Morcom intended to set to music.

Turing at Sherborne, aged about fifteen

But Morcom suffered from frequent illness and was often out of school. As a result they wrote long letters to one another, addressing each other as 'Dear Morcom' and 'Dear Turing' and discussing problems in physics, chemistry, maths and astronomy – their new passion.

In the summer of 1929, the boys took their Higher School Certificate. Morcom got high marks in the mathematics paper; Turing did not do so well. The examiner commented:

'A.M. Turing showed an unusual aptitude for noticing the less obvious points to be discussed or avoided in certain questions and for discovering methods which would at once shorten or illumine the solutions. But he appeared to lack the patience necessary for careful computation of algebraic verification, and his handwriting was so bad that he lost marks frequently – sometimes because his work is definitely illegible, and sometimes because his misreading his own writing led him to mistakes.'

Now eighteen, Morcom had set his sights on a scholarship to Trinity College, Cambridge, the top scientific college at England's leading scientific university. Though a year younger, Turing followed suit. They travelled up to London together where Turing was introduced to Morcom's mother, a sculptor who had a studio there. Then they were driven to Cambridge to sit the entrance examination. Morcom passed; Turing didn't.

Soon they were parted for the Christmas vacation. Resuming their correspondence over the holidays, Morcom wrote that he was making a spectrograph, a scientific instrument to study light. From a poorer background, with fewer means at his disposal, Turing made a map of the cosmos, sticking paper around an old spherical glass lampshade. He rose each morning at four o'clock to mark the positions of the stars and constellations on it.

The two of them followed the path of a comet, which Turing then plotted on his star chart. At the beginning of the next term, he took the resulting map to show Morcom. Three weeks into the term, Morcom fell ill again. This time he was rushed to a hospital in London by ambulance. After two operations and six weeks of pain, he died of tuberculosis. Turing had lost his only friend.

He wrote to his mother:

'I feel that I shall meet Morcom again somewhere and that there will be some work for us to do together as I believed there was for us to do here. Now that I am left to do it alone I must not let him down, but put as much energy into it, if not as much interest, as if he were still here. If I succeed I shall be more fit to enjoy his company than I am now.'

He said that it never occurred to him to make other friends – 'Morcom . . . made everyone seem so ordinary.'

Turing also wrote to Morcom's mother, who said that his letter helped her in grief more than anyone else's.

CHANNELLING GRIEF

In memory of their son, the Morcoms instituted the Christopher Morcom Prize for Natural Science, which Turing won in 1930 and 1931. Science master A.J.P. Andrews said of his 1930 award:

'I first realized what an unusual brain Alan had when he presented me with a paper on the reaction between iodic acid and sulphur dioxide. I had used the experiment as a "pretty" demonstration – but he had worked out the mathematics of it in a way that astonished me . . . I have always thought Alan and his friend Christopher Morcom were the two most brilliant boys I have ever taught.'

Turing continued punishing his body with his athletic endeavours. He won the house steeplechase and leapt the Tregudda Gorge while on holiday in Cornwall that summer. And in his grief he continued to channel his energies into science and mathematics. He began to learn German, though his teacher said: 'He does not seem to have any aptitude for languages.' But he was doing this for a reason. The next time he won a school prize, he asked for *Mathematische Grundlagen der Quantenmechanik* (The Mathematical Foundations of Quantum Mechanics), by John von Neumann.

Nor was he content with book-learning. On a sunny Sunday, he assembled a replica of Foucault's pendulum in the stairwell, a device that Jean-Bernard-Léon Foucault had used to demonstrate the rotation of the earth in 1851. Teachers and members of staff flocked to see it.

Turing was eventually made a prefect, though he soon turned against administering corporal punishment to younger boys. He then won the school's King Edward VI Gold Medal for Mathematics and a scholarship to study mathematics at Cambridge, which gave him £800 a year, twice the amount received by the unemployed in those years of the Depression. But first, he took an Officers' Training Corps course at Knightsbridge barracks. Excelling at drill and tactics, he demonstrated that he had the necessary strength and endurance to qualify as a reserve officer.

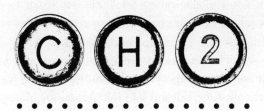

The Frontiers of Mathematics

Cambridge University was a haven for mathematicians. Isaac Newton had been professor of mathematics at the university from 1669 to 1701 and before the First World War Bertrand Russell had written *Principia Mathematica* there with Alfred North Whitehead.

Despite the influence of Morcom, Turing was still a sloppy dresser with few social skills and in his early days at Cambridge he made few friends. While he was generally considered an egghead, he did make the King's College rowing team. He was still a loner though, spending much of his spare time on long runs.

Emulating his idol Einstein, Turing bought a violin and taught himself to play. He also ran an experiment that involved the inter-breeding of fruit flies. During the vacation he took the flies home in test tubes, but they escaped and infested his luggage, then his parents' home. They were not amused.

FIRST SEXUAL RELATIONSHIP

Throughout his time at university Turing continued writing to Morcom's mother. But eventually he did make a new friend, whose name was David Champernowne. A fellow mathematics student, 'Champ' outshone Turing, publishing a paper when still an undergraduate. The poor standard of mathematics teaching at Sherborne left Turing with a great deal of catching up to do. Nevertheless he pleased his tutors with his unconventional approach, which often yielded results by simpler methods than those employed by others.

At Cambridge at that time, homosexuality – though illegal – was largely tolerated. It was generally assumed that public schoolboys were basically bisexual. Many who had youthful homosexual dalliances went on to marry and be solely heterosexual. Others would remain, or become, fully gay. Turing barely hid his interest in that quarter. The walls of his rooms were hung with pictures of young body-builders in swimming trunks, along with pictures of Morcom.

Somewhat reminiscent of Sebastian Flyte's teddy bear Aloysius in *Brideshead Revisited*, Turing asked his mother to send him a teddy, which he called Porgy, saying that he had not had one as a child.

To celebrate his twenty-first birthday, Turing went on a nine-day hike in the Lake District with a fellow maths student called James Atkins. On a hot summer's day, Turing seized the opportunity to sunbathe naked and they had sex.

A few days later, Turing went to Morcom's home to mark what would have been his dead friend's twenty-second birthday. Back in Cambridge, Turing's sexual relationship with Atkins resumed, on Atkins' initiative. However, Turing was unsure of himself and continued to maintain that he was not a homosexual.

'If you want to go to bed,' Turing told Atkins, 'it will be one-sided.'

POLITICAL PHASE

In the 1930s, the universities were a hotbed of politics. With Fascism and Nazism on the rise in Europe, the Communist Party found willing adherents. While Turing was at Cambridge, the Soviet Union recruited the infamous Cambridge spy ring – Kim Philby, Guy Burgess, Donald Maclean, Anthony Blunt and allegedly a fifth man, who went on to infiltrate MI6 and the Foreign Office. Turing too got swept up in the fervour of the times. In 1933, he wrote to his mother saying that he was thinking of going to Russia.

'I have joined an organization called the "Anti-War Council",' he went on. 'Politically rather Communist. Its programme is principally to organize strikes amongst munitions and chemical workers when the government intends to go to war. It gets up a guarantee fund to support the workers who strike.'

He joined a demonstration against the film *Our Fighting Navy*, which he condemned as 'blatant militarist propaganda'. Even so, he went on a cycling holiday to Germany in 1934 after the Nazis had come to power and was there during the 'Night of the Long Knives', when Hitler ordered the murder of some eighty-six leading members

The Front Court at King's College, Cambridge, where Turing enrolled as an undergraduate in 1931

of the party – many of them homosexuals – to secure his grip on power. Turing translated newspaper reports of the purge for other students and saw the Nazis at work. He heard of other student groups, particularly ones that included Jews, being beaten up. And when a travelling companion bid farewell to a German by saying 'Heil Hitler', he told him: 'You shouldn't have said that.'

CAMBRIDGE DON

Back in Cambridge Turing became aware of the influx of German-Jewish academics who were fleeing the Nazis and after what he had seen in Germany he turned away from pacifism.

In 1934, Turing graduated with distinction and King's College awarded him a research grant of £200. He had noticed in his scientific work that graphs depicting results tended to assume similar patterns. To discover the reason for this, he developed the Central Limit Theorem. He submitted this for a fellowship. However, the judges discovered that the theorem had been demonstrated by an Austrian mathematician named Kurt Gödel twelve years earlier. But they found Turing's proof superior and he was awarded a fellowship at £300 a year for three years. He was just twenty-two. When the news reached Sherborne, the clerihew circulated:

Turing
Must have been alluring
To get made a don
So early on.

After graduating Turing was no longer eligible for the rowing team and spent even more time running.

THE *ENTSCHEIDUNGSPROBLEM*

One day, resting in a field outside Grantchester, his mind turned to the *Entscheidungsproblem* – the decision-making problem – posed by

German mathematician David Hilbert. It boiled down to: Was there a test that would show whether any mathematical proposition was solvable? Hilbert believed that there was such a test and that it could be performed by an automatic machine. However, he did not go on to describe the machine.

Turing had attended a lecture on the *Entscheidungsproblem* by M.H.A. 'Max' Newman, who again raised the idea of the test being administered by some mechanical process. Outside Grantchester, Turing began in his mind to construct an imaginary problem-solving machine.

As a youth Turing had been a scientist before he became a mathematician, so he was a natural sceptic. He doubted Hilbert's contention which was, essentially, that there was no such thing as an insoluble problem.

One that easily sprang to mind was the so-called 'liar's paradox' first formulated by Epimenides of Knossos around 600BC. He said simply: 'All Cretans are liars.' But Epimenides himself was a Cretan. So if, as a Cretan, he is a liar, then what he says is untrue and all Cretans are truthful – so as a Cretan he must be telling the truth, in which case he is lying. And so on.

The liar's paradox remained a problem for mathematicians. The trouble started when Gottfried Leibniz posited that everything could be expressed as mathematical symbols, so disagreements could be solved by calculating the answers in the same way that problems in mathematics could be solved. The German philosopher Gottlob Frege sought to prove this in his masterwork *Grundgesetze* (Fundamental Laws) 1893. He was about to publish the second volume in 1903 when Bertrand Russell wrote to him, pointing out a hole in his assumptions.

There was a political dimension to this. Hilbert thought that a logical underpinning to everything would promote international harmony and peace, while Frege's views verged on the proto-fascist. Then in 1931 the Austrian mathematician Kurt Gödel holed the idea

Kurt Gödel (left) takes a walk with Albert Einstein around the campus at Princeton

again with his Incompleteness Theorem, which showed that any system that is consistent – like mathematics – cannot be complete. After the *Anschluss*, when Hitler's Germany annexed Austria in 1938, Gödel left for Princeton.

It was clear to Turing that there were plenty of mathematical problems that were thought to be unsolvable. But how could you tell which were solvable and which were not? Turing reasoned that the only way to find out was to try and solve them.

A mathematical proposition is conventionally expressed in the form of an equation. It has an input on the left-hand side and an output on the right-hand side. To solve the equation you take a series of specific steps, such as adding a number to, or subtracting it from, both sides, or multiplying or dividing both sides by the same quantity. This series of steps is called an algorithm. If any algorithm can be shown to give a definite result then the problem is solvable.

THE TURING MACHINE

Turing visualized a machine that applied an algorithm by going step-by-step through a series of simple operations – in the same way that a computer does these days. The simplest Turing machine is a paper tape divided into frames. Each frame is either filled in or is left blank – the equivalent of the 0s and 1s used by a modern digital computer. The tape is read by a scanner head that can either fill in a blank frame, erase the content if it is filled in, or do nothing, leaving the frame blank or filled in as it was before. The head would then move on to the left or the right. Turing then drew up a table of operations that the notional head would perform, one after the other. He realized that a rule table could be constructed for any solvable problem. However, even though this imaginary machine could indeed have, theoretically, an infinite capacity for calculation, Turing could show that some problems could not be solved by any rule table. So Hilbert was wrong. Not all problems were solvable.

More importantly, Turing proved that his machine could compute anything that could be computed. At first, he thought that there could be any number of Turing machines, each designed to do a specific task. Then he found that he could come up with rule tables that would make one machine mimic any other Turing machine. So there could be a single machine with a single rule table that could solve all solvable problems. This was what Turing called the Universal Machine, but which is generally known as a Turing machine.

Turing's Universal Machine was never built. It is a purely hypo-thetical device, existing only in the abstract, but it is the forerunner of every computer that came after it. Both the data and the instructions were notionally stored on paper tape, while the rules table was its operating system. Not only could it perform mathematical computations, it could handle any form of information that could be encoded as fill frames or blanks on paper tape.

In 1936, Turing wrote up his results in the paper 'On computable numbers with an application to the *Entscheidungsproblem*'. But before it could be published in *Proceedings of the London Mathematical Society* a paper arrived from Princeton. The American mathematician Alonzo Church had already cracked the decision-making problem and had published his results.

Church had used a completely different method to solve the *Entscheidungsproblem*. It was not as complete as Turing's method and Church had not argued from first principles as Turing had. So it was decided that the publication of Turing's paper should go ahead with Church as referee, as he was the only person qualified to perform the task. Normally only the first person to publish a new result gets the credit. But as Turing's method was so different from Church's, he got equal credit for what became known as the Church–Turing Thesis.

Max Newman wrote to Church asking him to take Turing on as a PhD student at Princeton. After visiting Mrs Morcom one last time, Turing set sail for America. His mother saw him off at Southampton.

97. 9 B A A 1A. B. O A   B 5 C 3
 82 8   707F25 A 7 9 A2 DD F 1 1A D9CO A
 5A446   04B27A1C E 3BCDE 81E89B. 4549BCDC3
    B827 9B8DBA89BA677D45FF8DF75A34AD
   7E0342ADC9672D8EE8F46FF90E63E2C061DC
 8AB90AA91DCE19EA87D45B827496 2C6 873 C8
 BA3087D38CBAB2B446FF0342AD9 9 AA 1E 8 1
 90472D8ADCCB3087D38AB245A6BA1B2B449ADA

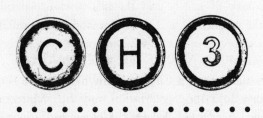

Calculating
Minds

42ADC1F25B430D9C00A6D8DF75A34F4129672D8EE8
A91DC06E97BEA6A8E13F2E62E2C061ADCE19EA8
7D38C89EA8707F25BADAC62C6EC8789FCBAB2B
  6BA1B2B4490AA91D4789C9BAA1E3F021DADCC
4F4161ADCCB3087D38AB27A8EE6137A1C389FCE034
  2BEB01 FF7BA8C878906E97BCDEA8E3F0290
 CA2 DF9 472 A1E3 89EA87D45FF38FD26D982
7A1 6E B349 C C6 37 A1B2B446FF907256E80B10
AB27A1C6EB33BCAB850CC89EA87D45FF7BA4AA0
 8DBA89BA675B430D9C0A1B2B446FF9047238
4AA1C6B4. 0D9. 003F2E6D248F6D 8C89EE85EC
 7A B7B A6A 1 AC 2 FB 0 BA1B 850C
A.2 E.7 7 2 .78 C 2   F .6 A D9

Turing took the Cunard liner *Berengaria* to New York. On board, he wrote to his mother saying:

'It strikes me that Americans can be the most insufferable and insensitive creatures you could wish. One of them has just been talking to me and telling me of the worst aspects of America with evident pride. However, they may not all be like that.'

APPLICATIONS OF MATHEMATICS

Despite his misgivings, Turing found himself very much at home at Princeton. Both the organization and the architecture of the university had been modelled on the older institutions at Oxford and Cambridge. The Institute for Advanced Study founded at Princeton in 1932 attracted many top scientists and mathematicians fleeing the Nazis. These included Albert Einstein and the Hungarian polymath John von Neumann, who quickly realized Turing's true stature. In von Neumann's eyes, Turing had created a new discipline – computability.

Turing got on well with Church, who proposed a programme of work for him, but he was already developing his ideas in a different direction. He wrote to his mother:

'You have often asked me about possible applications of various branches of mathematics. I have just discovered a possible application of the kind of thing I am working on at present. It answers the question "What is the most general kind of code or cipher possible?", and at the same time (rather naturally) enables me to construct a lot of particular and interesting codes. One of them is pretty well impossible to decode without

Fuld Hall, the main building at the Institute for Advanced Study

a key, and very quick to encode. I expect I could sell them to H.M. Government for quite a substantial sum, but am rather doubtful about the morality of such things. What do you think?'

Searching for practical applications for pure mathematics put Turing at odds with most other mathematicians, who believed that mathematics was a purely intellectual activity that should be completely divorced from the real world.

Even applied mathematics was then only being applied to highly theoretical topics such as relativity and quantum mechanics. Much later, quantum mechanics found itself at the heart of modern computers, but it was important for the generation who lived in the shadow of the First World War that mathematics should not be seen to have any warlike applications.

SOCIAL LIFE

Although Turing remained very much a loner, he did participate in some social activities, even playing hockey against a women's team at Vassar. Church occasionally invited him out to dinner, but he found the conversation with other academics boring. He became friends with a young American student named Venable Martin. They went out canoeing together and Turing 'indirectly indicated' an interest in having a homosexual relationship. Martin made it clear that he was not gay. Nevertheless, the two remained firm friends.

Despite this rejection, Turing was happy in his work. He wrote to his mother: 'The mathematics department here comes fully up to expectations. There are a great number of the most distinguished mathematicians here.'

DISTINGUISHED COMPANY

In his letter, Turing mentioned Einstein, whom he saw occasionally in the corridors. But, like Turing, Einstein kept himself to himself. The publication of Turing's paper describing the Universal Machine did not attract much attention on either side of the Atlantic and few people turned out for his lecture on the subject. Its lukewarm reception depressed Turing and he dealt with his depression, as before, by running. Now he began running against the clock with the aim of, one day, competing in the Olympics.

Turing also considered suicide. In a letter to James Atkins, he described a plan to end his life that involved an apple and electrical wiring, Atkins recalled later.

Von Neumann presented Turing with a problem in group theory, which he solved speedily. He then decided to stay on at Princeton for another year. But first he returned to Cambridge for three months, where he had to correct errors in his paper that had been published in the London Mathematical Society's *Proceedings*. A correction note was added. He then began work on a problem with prime numbers. He wanted to explain that while there are an infinite number of them

John von Neumann stands next to an early computer at the Institute for Advanced Study in the late 1940s

they become rarer the higher you go. During his stay, he became acquainted with the Viennese philosopher Ludwig Wittgenstein. A Jewish intellectual who had been at school with Adolf Hitler, he had become a fellow of Trinity College in 1929. Having been trained in early life as an engineer, Wittgenstein appreciated Turing's Universal Machine, but disagreed profoundly with his conclusions, believing that every well-posed problem had a solution.

Turing spent a weekend with Atkins in London. They went to see Elmer Rice's play *Judgment Day*, which is about the Reichstag fire that consolidated Hitler's hold on power. Despite his anti-Nazi sentiments, Turing travelled back to America on board the German liner *Europa*, as it was faster than the other passenger ships plying the Atlantic. On the way, though, he spent his time learning Russian, enjoying the look of shock on the German passengers' faces when he wielded a textbook emblazoned with a hammer and sickle. Also on board was a friend from graduate college, Will Jones from Mississippi. Back in Princeton, they spent their time discussing philosophy.

NUMBER CODE IDEA

In the autumn of 1937, Turing began to fear that there would be another war between Britain and Germany, and started to work again on codes. His idea was that words would be replaced by numbers taken from a code book. These numbers would then be multiplied by a secret number before being transmitted. That way the enemy would not be able to decipher the message even if they had the code book. But how long should the secret number be? Turing's self-imposed specification was that it should take a hundred Germans working eight hours a day with desk calculators a hundred years to discover it by a routine search.

As part of this work, Turing designed an electric multiplying machine and built the first three or four stages. The electrical relays it needed were not commercially available, so he made them himself in the workshop at Princeton. As in his Universal Machine, Turing's electric multiplier used binary numbers. This time he also introduced Boolean algebra. Formulated in 1854, it uses the operators AND, OR and NOT, which are key elements in modern computing. As he worked on his multipliers, it became clear to him that he could use the circuitry to make an electric Universal Machine.

In fact, Turing's idea for a number code was useless. Firstly, the Germans could simply look for the highest common factor between two numbers and use it as the key. And if a single digit was transmitted incorrectly, the whole message would be indecipherable.

When Turing finished his PhD, von Neumann asked him to stay at Princeton as his assistant. With war imminent, Turing's father urged him to remain in America, but Turing decided to return to King's. He arrived in Southampton on board the *Normandie*. He was carrying his electric multiplier mounted on a breadboard and wrapped up in a brown paper bag.

97. 9 B A A 1 A . B . O A   B 5 C 3
82 8 707F25 A 7 9 A2 DD F. 1 1A D9C0 A
.5A446   04B27A1C E 3BCDE 81E89B. 4549BCDC3
 B827 9B8DBA89BA677D45FF8DF75A34AD
7E0342ADC9672D8EE8F46FF90E62E2C061DC
8AB90AA91DCE19EA87D45B8274962C6 C8738C8
BA3087D38CBAB2B446FF0342AD9 89 AA 1E8BA1
90472D8ADCCB3087D38AB245A6BA1B2B449ADA.

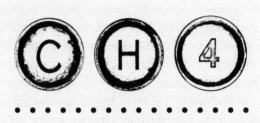

CH 4

• • • • • • • • • • • • • •

Enigma

42ADC1F25B430D9C00A6D8DF75A34F4129672D8EE8
A91DC06E97BEA6A8E13F2E62E2C061ADCE19EA8
7D38C89EA8707F25BADAC62C6EC8789FCBAB2B
 6BA1B2B4490AA91D4789C9BAA1E3F021DADCC
4F4161ADCCB3087D38AB27A8EE6137A1C389FCE034
2BEB010FF7BA8C878906E97BCDEA8E3F0290
CA2 0DF9 472 1E3 89EA87D45FF38FD26D982
7A1 6EB349 C C613 A1B2B446FF907256E80B10
AB27A1C6EB33BCAB850CC89EA87D45FF7BA4AA0
 8DBA89BA675B430D9C0A1B2B446FF9047238
4AA1C6B4. 0D9. 003F2E6D248F6D 8C89EE85EC
 7A B7B A6A 1 AC 2 FB 0 BA1B 850C
A.2 E.772 . 78 C 2   F .6 A D9

By the time Turing returned from Princeton, Britain was preparing for war. 'Will be seeing you in the middle of July,' he had written to his supervisor at King's, Philip Hall, 'I also expect to find the back lawn criss-crossed with 8ft. trenches.' It had not come to that, but behind the scenes the wheels of war were turning.

BLETCHLEY PARK ACQUIRED

Codebreaking would play a vital part in the Second World War, as it had in the First World War. In 1914, Russia gave the British a captured German code book and a large number of wireless and telegraph messages were broken, largely by civilian staff recruited from universities. They were housed in Room 40 in the Admiralty building in Whitehall. In 1917, the British intercepted a coded telegram from the German foreign minister. It proposed that if the United States entered the war on the side of the Allies, the Germans would encourage Mexico to declare war on the United States and take back their lost territories of Texas, New Mexico and California. When its contents were exposed, it caused such outrage that the United States finally came into the war on the Allies' side.

After the carpet bombing of the Spanish city of Guernica in 1937 by Germany's Luftwaffe, during the Spanish Civil War, it was clear that Germany had a powerful bomber force. In any war against Britain, the government buildings around Whitehall were an obvious target. With the huge increase in military communication, a large number of codebreakers would be required and they should be moved somewhere safe. A country house outside the small town of Bletchley in Buckinghamshire was found. It was 400 yards from the station and was surrounded by 580 acres of farmland, meadows and woods. This would be the new home of the Government Code and Cypher School (GC&CS). Post Office engineers discreetly installed a mass of new telephone lines and the grounds were

Bletchley Park near Milton Keynes, which became the headquarters of the Government Code and Cypher School during the Second World War

patrolled by 'shooting parties'. A top-secret installation, it was known only as Station X.

GC&CS were interested in Turing's Universal Machine and the mind behind it. Even before he went to Princeton, they had approached him. When he returned, they contacted him again.

It was clear that Europe was plunging headlong into war. Italy had invaded Abyssinia (Ethiopia) and had signed a pact with Germany, which had then taken over Austria and Czechoslovakia. After returning to England, Turing was personally involved in the conflict.

'Though he had little more than the salary of a Fellow,' his mother wrote, 'just before the Second World War he made himself responsible for all the expenses, except school fees, of an Austrian refugee of fifteen. As self-constituted guardian of the boy, Alan paid for all his clothing, holidays and extras, and later paid all his expenses at Manchester University.'

ECCENTRIC GOINGS-ON

On 4 September 1939, the day after war was declared, Turing arrived at Bletchley Park. He was billeted in the Crown Inn three miles to the north and cycled back and forth wearing a gas mask in summer, as he suffered badly from hay fever. He also served behind the Crown Inn bar to eke out his wartime salary.

The local people somewhat resented the denizens of Bletchley Park, thinking that people of their age should be in uniform. The local MP had to be stopped from asking a question in Parliament.

To deflect criticism, the academics at Bletchley Park were dragooned into the Home Guard and spent nights in the surrounding fields watching for German parachutists. Turing leapt at the idea of joining the Home Guard as it would give him an opportunity to learn how to shoot. As it turned out, he was a rather good marksman. But once he had perfected his shooting skills his enthusiasm waned and he began to absent himself from parades. The authorities were annoyed by Turing's lax approach, and an officer pointed out that when he had signed up he had put himself under military law.

Turing's assistant, Peter Twinn, said that Turing had anticipated this situation when he joined the Home Guard.

'They told him to fill this form in and Turing thought to himself: "I don't see why I should sign this. It won't do me any good and it might be a bit inconvenient." So when he had learned how to fire a rifle and done as much as he thought was of value to him, he thought: "Well, I've got everything I can out of this, I'll just give up going to the Home Guard." When the officer in charge said he would do what he was told because he had agreed to be subject to military discipline, Turing replied, and I can hear him saying it: "Well, you had better look at my form. You'll see I didn't sign that bit."'

The eccentric Turing was hardly out of place in Bletchley Park's Home Guard. Intelligence Corps officer Noel Currer-Briggs recalled that at one point a mixture of the Home Guard and the regular army marched into Bletchley as part of a recruiting campaign.

'There were a bunch of oddballs there, people from all over Europe with obscure languages,' he said. 'There was one chap from Eastern Europe in battledress and a bowler hat, much to the dismay of the sergeant who was trying to make us look smart. It made *Dad's Army* look like the Coldstream Guards.'

As it was, the goings-on there do not seem to have been as secret as the top brass might have hoped. When one senior crypt-analyst arrived at the station, a little boy cried out: 'I'll read your secret writing, mister.'

TURING'S TASK

Turing's task at Bletchley Park, along with that of fellow Cambridge mathematician Gordon Welchman, was to break the German Enigma code. In the run-up to the war, the two of them had attended short courses in cryptography organized by GC&CS and they set to work on pre-war traffic. Quite independently, Turing managed to break five days' worth of Enigma material. This was encouraging, but no one at Bletchley Park had yet had any success with current German traffic.

British success in the First World War had proved to the Germans the importance of secure communication. Even before the end of the war the German inventor Arthur Scherbius had patented a design for a machine that could encrypt secret messages. He approached the German navy and the foreign office, but they turned him down as they had still not realized that their codes had been broken. However, in 1923 he began selling machines to banks. The German navy bought a few and some were sold to various foreign diplomatic services.

German electrical engineer Arthur Scherbius, the inventor of the original Enigma machine

THE ENIGMA MACHINE

Scherbius died in 1929 and his company stopped trading commercially when the Nazis came to power in 1933. However, the factory was expanded and it began producing Enigma machines solely for military use. The commercial machines Scherbius had designed were models A to D. An Enigma-G had been designed for the army. Now an upgraded version – Enigma-I, also known as the Service Enigma – went into production.

It came in a wooden case a foot long, eleven inches wide and six inches high and had a typewriter keyboard with a standard German layout. QWERTZUIO appeared on the top row of keys instead of the QWERTYUIOP found on a standard Anglo-American keyboard. P and Y appear on the bottom row of keys. Above the keyboard was a matching panel of letters and each letter had a light underneath it. Above that the notched edges of three rotors protruded through slots. Opening the front panel revealed a plugboard with twenty-six numbered sockets. These could be connected together by short cables that had a plug at each end. The rotors and the plugboard together produced an immensely complicated code which the Germans thought was unbreakable.

The simplest code is a straight substitution of a letter for the one that follows it in the alphabet – so A becomes B, B becomes C, and so on. A variation on this is a keyword code, where you use a word in which there are no repeated letters – such as CODE – as your starting point. So A, B, C and D become C, O, D and E. The rest of the alphabet is encoded with the letters you haven't already used. So E becomes A, F becomes B, G becomes F, H becomes G . . . Clues could be provided by the length of the words. A single letter would be A or I, two letters would be TO, or OF, or ON, or AS, or OR. So the message is broken up into, say, groupings of five letters.

Even so, a straight substitution code is relatively simple to break. For example, E is the most commonly used letter in the English language, so if a T appears most frequently in a message it is likely to be an E. The frequency with which each letter appears in each language is well known. If a message is over a hundred letters long, it is possible to work out more than half of them using this method. The rest can be inferred from the context, or just guessed.

An advance on this was to use two concentric rings. The inner ring has the alphabet in order on it; the outer has the letters jumbled. The chosen letter on the inner ring is then encoded as the one opposite it on the outer ring. But after each letter is encoded, the ring is advanced one character. In effect, each letter is being encrypted using a different code and the message can only be decoded by someone who has an identical set of discs. But if the enemy captured a set of discs, they could read the code. They would not know the starting position, but they would only have to try a maximum of twenty-six times before the message came out in clear language.

What Scherbius had done was to take this simple idea and multiply the number of starting points. When a key is pressed on an Enigma machine, a switch is closed which allows the current to run through the three different rotors and activate one of the lights under the letters on the lamp panel. This is written down by the operator. Each of the twenty-six inputs on the rotors is connected to a different output. The contacts on the first rotor make a connection with those on the second rotor, which make a connection with those on the third rotor, each time substituting one letter for another. The key-press also advances the rotors so that the next letter will be encoded using a different set of substitutions.

The message can be further encrypted by using the plugboard which is connected to the contacts on the entry wheel, a static wheel that makes a connection with the first of the rotors after making a substitution of its own. If nothing is plugged into the socket equivalent to A, it will be passed on as an A. But if A is connected to the socket equivalent to T, then a T is sent on. This itself can produce up to 200 million million possibilities – though, of course, this would be a straight substitution which could be broken by letter-frequency analysis if it weren't for the rotors.

The original machine came with three rotors, marked I, II and III. Each of the twenty-six contacts on the right-hand side is wired to a different contact on the left-hand side. On rotor I, A is connected to E, B to K, C to M, and so on. On rotors II and III, contacts are wired in different orders.

The rotors themselves can be loaded into the machine in a different order, giving six possibilities in all. The outer rings that protrude through the slots are notched and each can be set up in twenty-six different positions. A letter appears in a little window in the case of the navy Enigma machine, a number in the army and air force versions. With three rotors there are 105,456 possible starting positions.

Once the current has passed through all three rotors it hits the reflector. This is another fixed disc with the twenty-six contacts wired together in pairs, so the current passes out of the reflector and back through the rotor again. It reaches a different contact on the entry rotor, which passes it back through the plugboard and then to the light. Then the key is released.

When the next key is pressed, the first rotor is advanced one twenty-sixth of a turn, changing the configuration of the circuit through the machine. So if an A was pressed the first time and lit up a P, the second time it might light up a J, a third time a Q. Every twenty-six keystrokes, a pin on the first rotor advances the second rotor one letter and if the message is over 676 characters long a pin on the second rotor advances the third rotor one letter.

The unit receiving the message simply had to set up the machine in exactly the same way as the sender's, type in the coded message and wait for clear text to come out. But for anyone trying to break the code there were a staggering 107,458,491,300,000,000,000,000 possibilities. This was the code Turing was to crack. But he did not have to start from scratch.

THE POLISH CRYPTANALYSTS

In the 18th century, Poland had been partitioned by Russia, Prussia and Austria. It had only been reconstituted again as a nation in 1918, but it remained constantly under threat from its large neighbours, Russia and Germany. Like other governments, the Poles had bought commercial Enigma machines from Scherbius in the 1920s, so they knew how they worked. However, the new Service Enigma machines were wired differently.

In 1932, three mathematicians from Poznan University named Marian Rejewski, Henryk Zygalski and Jerzy Różycki joined the

Polish Cipher Bureau and began working on the Enigma code. French military intelligence passed them some stolen German documents which included two sheets containing the daily Enigma settings for a month. By using enciphered messages and the settings the French had given them, Rejewski managed to work out the wiring inside the rotors and reflector of the military device. With that knowledge, they managed to build a replica Enigma machine.

This did not mean they could crack the code, because they did not know what the current start-up settings were. All they could do was type in the start of the message and see if it came out as gibberish. If it did, they would have to change the settings. However with 107,458,491,300,000,000,000,000 possibilities, it was unlikely that they would run across the right combination in a lifetime. Even today, using supercomputers, it would take a couple of days to hit on the combination that would turn the encoded message into clear text. With the even more complex U-boat Enigma code that Turing broke, a supercomputer would take several years.

As there was a vanishingly small chance of hitting on the right combination by trial and error, the Poles took another approach. They studied the German operating procedures, looking for flaws. The daily settings included three letters. The Enigma machine was set up with these three letters in the rotor windows. The operator would then pick three other letters, encode them on the machine and send them, then reset the machine with the new letters and send the message.

The operator on the receiving end would have his machine set up using the same daily settings. When he received the three new letters the sender had transmitted he would decipher them and then reset his Enigma machine using the decrypted letters, before going on to decipher the rest of the message.

However, because of poor radio reception the three new letters would be sent twice, though the Enigma machine would encode them differently. But knowing that letters one and four were the same, as were letters two and five, and three and six, was enough to cut down the possible settings to hundreds of thousands. With his knowledge of the wiring patterns, Rejewski built up a card index using these initial six-letter groupings. He then designed a machine to speed up the selection process and found that he could identify the rotor order for that day within a quarter of an hour. That did not break the code completely and there was still the contribution of the plugboard to decipher. But that generated a straightforward substitution code which could be broken by letter-frequency analysis.

Things were going smoothly enough until November 1937, when the Germans issued a new reflector that was wired differently. The operating instructions were amended to say which reflector was to be used that day. Guessing what had happened, Rejewski spent a year building an index for the new reflector.

This only worked for the army and the air force. Already in May 1937, the German navy, the Kriegsmarine, had stopped sending messages as text. Instead it had a code book that translated all standard messages into a four-figure code. The numbers were then translated into letters using a straightforward substitution code, then encoded on to the Enigma machine. That meant that even if the Poles got the right settings on their replica Enigma machine the message would not come out as plain text, so they would not know if they had broken the code.

In May 1938 the German army and air force also tightened their procedures, adding a further set of three letters chosen by the operator. But operators were sloppy. Famously, one operator had a girlfriend call Cilli and always used the same three letters – 'CIL'. There were other clues. Sometimes there would be a repeated letter in the same position in both of the new three-letter settings the operator was sending. These were called 'females' because of a woman's double X chromosome and this again limited the possibilities.

Zygalski came up with an ingenious method of trawling through the various possibilities using females. He produced a stack of twenty-six sheets each with holes cut in them to represent the rotor settings. These were manipulated until you could see through a hole in the top ones down to those below. Gradually those that aligned would slim down to only one. After that the settings of the plugboard could be worked out by frequency analysis and that day's code was broken.

But six stacks of sheets were needed, one for each possible order of the rotors, and Zygalski had only made two. Then the Germans added two new rotors, IV and V. The operating instructions were amended again, telling the operator which three rotors to use out of the five. There were now sixty possible rotor configurations, so sixty stacks of sheets would be needed.

Meanwhile, Rejewski had reasoned that as the code had been generated by a machine it could be broken by a machine. Again the search would be narrowed by searching for females. He built six triple drums, one for each rotor order, wired up in a way that was analogous to the rotors in the Enigma machine. The drums would spin until a circuit was made. The relevant drum would then stop with a loud bang and the setting would be read off. It was, perhaps, the noise the drum made when it came to a halt that gave it the name *bomba kryptologiczna*, or 'cryptological bomb'. Or the *bomba* could have been named after an ice cream popular in Poland at the time.

A complete search for the initial settings on three rotors could be done in two hours. Thanks to a mistake made by the German Security Services, the SD, the Poles managed to figure out the wiring on the new rotors, but they did not have the resources to build the sixty *bombas* they were now going to need. However, they were miles ahead of the British, who were still where the Poles had been in 1932.

DESIGNING THE BOMBE

In July 1939 there had been a secret meeting between British, French and Polish cryptanalysts in Warsaw. Until then, no one in the British delegation had even thought of the possibility of using a high-speed machine to analyse the Enigma codes. Turing was particularly impressed. He noted that Zygalski was cutting his sheets by hand. In England, Turing found a printer's shop capable of perforating the sheets. Sixty sets were run off and Bletchley Park set to work with one of Rejewski's replica Enigma machines.

With Germany invading Poland from the west, followed by the Soviets from the east, Rejewski, Zygalski and Różycki escaped via Romania to France and went to work at an intercept station near Paris. This was connected by telegraph to Bletchley Park and messages were exchanged using replica Enigmas and signed off with, ironically, 'Heil Hitler'.

Turing and Welchman soon spotted that the Enigma would not encode a letter as itself. Consequently, if they guessed at stock phrases that the Germans were likely to use in messages – which they called 'cribs' – they could run these along a line of encoded traffic to find the places where no letters matched. This again limited the possibilities and Turing now had a full set of Zygalski sheets to work with. But checking the possibilities this way proved too slow. With his interest in machines, Turing thought Rejewski's *bombas* were the obvious answer.

A Universal Machine, of course, would have been able to break the Enigma code – and a lot more besides. But it had not been built and Champernowne said that if it had been it would have needed the Albert Hall to house it. But the *bomba* was something that could be built and Turing immediately set about a new design. The *bomba* depended on the repeated setting at the beginning of the message and Turing feared that the Germans would soon spot this weakness and change their procedures. He also wanted to increase the speed. While Rejewski's *bombas* could break the code in a couple of hours when there had only been three rotors, now there were five it would take almost a day.

Although he had some experience from building his electrical multiplier, Turing was a mathematician not an engineer. But not far away in Letchworth was the British Tabulating Machine Company, which initially sold imported adding machines made by the US Tabulating Machine Company and went on to become IBM. BTM

A rear view of a 'bombe' code-breaking machine, photographed at Bletchley Park in 1943

had begun to manufacture their own adding machines and sorters, so their chief engineer, Harold 'Doc' Keen, was in a position to turn Turing's sketches into a working machine. The British version was called a bombe.

The result was a huge machine six-and-a-half feet tall, seven feet long and two feet wide. It weighed over a ton, with thirty-six 'scramblers' each emulating an Enigma machine and 108 drums selecting the possible key settings. Each of these was colour-coded to show which of the Enigma rotors it emulated. The machine's own plugboard allowed 'menus' to be chosen, gleaned from the use of cribs.

The young mathematician Oliver Lawn was sent to Letchworth to oversee the production. He said:

'Alan Turing was the theoretician, Welchman was the practical chap. And the two put together their brainpower and evolved his machine which was made in large quantities in Letchworth by the British Tabulating Machine Company, as it was then called.'

THE BOMBE ARRIVES

While the first bombe was under construction, Turing visited the Poles outside Paris and gave them a set of Zygalski sheets. They set to work codebreaking. Within a few days they had managed to crack the Enigma code again. Rejewski recalled his dealings with Turing: 'We treated Alan Turing as a younger colleague who had specialized in mathematical logic and was just starting out in cryptology.' He was unaware that Turing had already made some startling breakthroughs on his own account.

On 10 March 1940, just before the German army marched into Belgium, Luxembourg and Holland, the message traffic went dark once more. As Turing had feared, the Germans had stopped sending the double setting at the beginning of the message and the Polish method of breaking the Enigma code no longer worked.

The first bombe, named Victory, arrived at Bletchley Park on 18 March 1940. It cost £6,500, one-tenth of the price of a Lancaster bomber and around £100,000 today. It was also some 300,000 times faster than Rejewski's machine. But already Turing was working on plans to make a machine that was faster still.

Like the Polish model, the drums spun until a circuit was made. At that point the machine shuddered to a halt and the settings were read off. These were then used to set up a replica Enigma machine to see if plain text in German came out. If it did not, the machine was restarted.

Unless the crib was long – over 150 letters – there were a large number of false stops. Welchman solved the problem by adding a 'diagonal board'. This used the fact that the connecting wires on the plugboard in the Enigma machine joined pairs of letters, so if A was connected to D, D was connected to A. Turing quickly realized that

Welchman's diagonal board allowed them to do simultaneous scanning of all the possible twenty-six plugboard settings.

'Otherwise the best we could do with the first British bombe, as with the Polish ones, was to assume that the letter chosen as the input was unplugged, with a probability of six in twenty-six of this being correct,' said Joan Clarke, a Cambridge mathematician recruited by Welchman then running Hut 6. But on seeing the innovation:

'Turing soon jumped up, saying that Welchman's diagonal board would provide simultaneous scanning, and he hurried round to Hut 6 to give the good news, doubtless with a circuit diagram to explain the method of testing. When he showed it to me, he had to tell me how relays worked.'

97. 9 B A A 1A B 0 A B 5 C 3
82 8. 707F25 A 7 9 A2 DD F 1 1A D9C0 A
5A446 04B27A1C E 3BCDE 81E89B. 4549BCDC3
B827 9B8DBA89BA677D45FF8DF75A34AD
7E0342ADC9672D8EE8F46FF90E62E2C061DC
8AB90AA91DCE19EA87D45B827496̲2C6̲E̲C873̲9C8
BA3087D38CBAB2B446FF0342AD9̲C9̲B̲AA̲1E8BA̲1
90472D8ADCCB3087D38AB245A6BA1B2B449ADA

CH5

Enigma
Variations

42ADC1F25B430D9C00A6D8DF75A34F4129672D8EE8
A91DC06E97BEA6A8E13F2E62E2C061ADCE19EA8
7D38C89EA8707F25BADAC62C6EC8789FCBAB2B
6BA1B2B4490AA91D4789C9BAA1E3F021DADCC
4F4161ADCCB3087D38AB27A8EE6137A1C389FCE034
2BFB010FF7BA8C878906E97BCDEA8E3F0290
C̲A2̲9̲0DF9̲0472̲1̲A1E3̲F89EA87D45FF38FD26D982
7A1̲6̲E̲B349̲8C̲C̲013̲A1B2B446FF907256E80B10
AB27A1C6EB33BCAB850CC89EA87D45FF7BA4AA0
8DBA89BA675B430D9C0A1B2B446FF9047238
4AA1C6B4. 0D9. 003F2E6D248F6D 8C89EE85EC
7A B7B A6A 1 AC 2 FB 0 BA1B 850C
A 2 E.772 78 C 2 F .6 A D9

The Germans moved on through Belgium into France. Paris fell on 14 June 1940 and Rejewski, Zygalski and Różycki fled south. They continued their work in Algeria and unoccupied France, which was then run by the collaborator government under Marshal Pétain in the spa town of Vichy. Różycki drowned when the passenger ship on which he was returning from Algeria was sunk. Rejewski and Zygalski eventually escaped via Spain to Britain, but as they had spent time in Vichy France they were considered a security risk. However, they then joined the Polish army, where they continued their work cracking SS and SD codes.

AGGIE ARRIVES

Victory was still taking too long to find the rotor and plug settings. Every hour lost meant that a U-boat was six miles closer to a convoy. Turing realized that sometimes during the encryption of one message the rotors would be in the same position as the start position of another. To look for matches, he had messages punched into large index cards. One message card was laid on top of a second on a light box, which made it easier to detect repeats. The cards were printed in nearby Banbury, so they were known as Banburies and the process was known as Banburismus.

In August 1940 a second bombe arrived, with Welchman's diagonal board already fitted. This one was called 'Agnus Dei' ('Lamb of God') but was universally known as Aggie. Meanwhile Victory returned to the factory in Letchworth to have a diagonal board installed. At the time, the Battle of Britain was raging and the German codes were being broken at Bletchley Park, allowing the British to direct their fighters against incoming German bombers. When the battle was won, Bletchley Park intercepted messages cancelling the planned invasion of Britain.

CRACKING THE GERMAN NAVY'S CODE

But Britain was not out of danger yet. At the beginning of the war, the Royal Navy managed to keep the Kriegsmarine and its powerful U-boat fleet largely holed up in its home ports. But with the fall of France, massive bomb-proof submarine pens were built around the Bay of Biscay. The U-boats had direct access to the Atlantic without having to run the gauntlet of the English Channel or the North Sea. Cut off from the Continent, the North Atlantic was Britain's lifeline with food, fuel, raw materials and armaments coming in from the United States and the Empire.

The Royal Navy's sonar system – Asdic – could only detect a submarine if it was within 2,000 yards of the ship. It was next to useless when faced with the 41 million square miles of the North Atlantic, so it was vital that the more complex naval Enigma code was broken. Hopes were not high. The commander of Bletchley Park, Alastair Denniston, said to the head of the Naval Section, Frank Birch: 'You know, the Germans don't mean you to read their stuff, and I don't suppose you ever will.'

'Turing thought it could be broken because it would be so interesting to break it,' recalled Hugh Alexander, who worked alongside him. 'Turing first got interested in the problem for the typical reason that "no one else was doing anything about it and I could have it to myself".'

The German navy was using a standard Enigma machine. But instead of having just three or five rotors, it had eight. Three extra rotors – VI, VII and VIII – had been added. With three out of the eight being used, the possible combinations had been increased from sixty to 336. This meant that there were now 6,017,675,512,800,000,000,000,000 possible settings. The task of breaking the code seemed impossible. Even worse, the messages were then super-encrypted when the output of the Enigma machine was encoded a second time, this time by hand using 'bigram tables', which Turing set about reconstructing.

The German operator would pick three letters at random as the starting positions for the rotors – ASC, say. These would be encoded

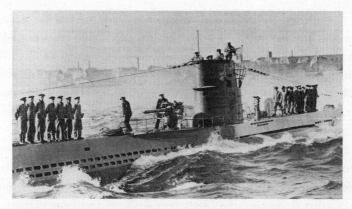

The crew of a German U-boat line up on deck c.1939

twice using the daily settings, so ASCASC would become, perhaps, LQRCPY. Then he would write them in this pattern:

L   Q   R
     C   P   Y

Two letters would be chosen at random to complete the rectangle, giving:

L   Q   R   T
O   C   P   Y

Then he would encrypt the vertical digraphs LO, QC, RP and TY using the bigram tables. There were ten of these in use for up to a year. Which one was to be used was given in the daily settings. LO might become TU, QC might become AH, RP might become LS and TY might become IU. The rectangle would then become:

T   A   L   I
U   H   S   U

The operator would then transmit TALI UHSU and the person receiving the key would reverse the procedure. The bigram tables were reciprocal, so if LO becomes TU, then TU becomes LO. After eliminating the two added letters, it was easy to check that there were no mistakes as the first two letters were repeated. They would then be used by both sender and receiver to set the rotors. This added a whole new level of difficulty for the codebreakers.

However, navy Enigma machines and code books were more vulnerable than those used by the German army and air force. While Wehrmacht and Luftwaffe Enigma machines were safe in their land bases often far behind the lines, the navy machines were out at sea and the Royal Navy was under strict instructions to board enemy shipping and seize cryptographic material. These windfalls were known at Bletchley Park as 'pinches'.

On 26 April 1940, HMS *Griffin* intercepted a German trawler sailing under a Dutch flag and carrying munitions off Narvik, northern Norway. The boat was *Schiff 26*, erroneously identified as *VP2623* in some accounts. One of the boarding party noticed a canvas bag in the water and jumped in to get it. He almost drowned, but the bag was found to contain the operator's log board containing messages in plain text – perfect cribs – and the plugboard settings and starting positions for 23–24 April. Using these, Turing's team in Hut 8 managed to crack six days' traffic by June.

ENGAGED TO BE MARRIED

Three of the days were cracked by Joan Clarke. At night they worked together on the bombes and she and Turing became briefly engaged. Like everyone else, though, she still called him 'Prof', even when a genuine professor was working there.

He was not much of a catch. One colleague at Bletchley said that Turing looked like 'a tramp'. Sometimes he appeared in the office in his pyjamas, or wore trousers held up by a striped necktie instead of a belt. His hair was unkempt and he had a permanent five o'clock shadow, refusing to shave with anything but an ancient electric razor. Though he did not smoke, his teeth were yellow and he bit his finger-nails to the point where there were small scars on the tips of his fingers. He was also a workaholic.

'I can remember Alan Turing coming in as usual for a day's leave,' said Joan, 'doing his own mathematical research at night, in the warmth and light of the office, without interrupting the routine of daytime sleep.'

Unlike most of the other women at Bletchley Park, Joan was a mathematician and Turing did not talk down to her. They would go to the cinema together, play tennis and chess and have long discus-sions about the Fibonacci sequence and its recurrence in nature. They continued to work closely together.

According to Joan:

'Turing wrote an account – "Prof's Book" – Enigma theory and methods, which were still largely experimental. Doubtless this was used to introduce later cryptanalysts to the work, although much of it was not needed in Hut 8. One chapter explained a method which could have recovered the wheel-wirings as well as the plugging, on material such as that from the captured German patrol boat *VP2623*. I was the guinea pig, to test whether his explanation and worked example were understand-able, and my task included using this method on half the material, not used in the example.'

Prof's Book was more formally entitled *Treatise on the Enigma*. It runs to 142 pages and is held in the National Archives, though a version can be found online in The Turing Digital Archive.

Despite Turing's sexual feelings for other men, it was common at the time for homosexuals to marry. Indeed, when Turing proposed to Joan, he mentioned his homosexual tendencies, without going into detail. She did not consider this a problem. He gave her an engagement ring and they met each other's parents. It was clear that, at last, Turing was ready to fulfil all the social norms.

ECCENTRICITIES

After the Narvik pinch, things went quiet until a Naval Intelligence officer, Lieutenant Commander Ian Fleming – later the creator of James Bond – came up with a daring plan. A captured German bomber would be crashed in the Channel near a suitable German vessel. The British crew in German uniforms – 'add blood and bandages to suit' wrote Fleming – would be on board. When they were rescued by the German vessel, they would kill the crew and take the ship, with its Enigma machine and code books, to a British port. The plan was named Operation Ruthless and as a German speaker Fleming planned to take the leading role. He even visited Bletchley Park. But reconnaissance flights failed to find a suitable target and when the operation was cancelled Turing and his assistant Peter Twinn were said to be 'like undertakers cheated of a nice corpse'.

Twinn recognized Turing as a genius.

'He was easily the brightest chap in the place. But he would occasionally come round to my digs and play chess and I should think that out of five games, he would win three and I would win two. But I knew very little about chess apart from the rules. I knew absolutely nothing about the tactics or strategy. It always seemed to me extraordinary that this brilliant chap was absolutely no good at chess at all. It was only because he hadn't given it his attention of course, but it was a rather curious phenomenon.'

He did turn his attention to it later and made up for this deficiency. Turing had also learned to play another game, Go, at Princeton and took on the Americans when they visited Bletchley Park later.

Twinn noted Turing's other eccentricities. As well as riding his bike wearing his gas mask, Turing chained his tea mug to the radiator. People would pick the lock and steal the mug just to tease him. He wore unpressed clothes, had a nervous habit of picking the skin around his fingernails and was painfully shy. Others mention his high-pitched voice, his hesitating stammer, the laugh that would grate on the nerves of even those closest to him and his habit of concluding any conversation by sidling out of the room with his eyes lowered, murmuring his thanks. Secretary Mimi Gallilee recalled often seeing him 'walking along the path – intense – always looking worried. People thought he was a bit of a weirdo'. Today, he would be diagnosed as having borderline Asperger's syndrome.

HOW OTHERS SAW TURING

Chess players were much valued in Hut 8. British chess champion Harry Golombek, who became chess correspondent for *The Times* from 1945 to 1989, was recruited. When 18-year-old Oxford undergraduate Peter Hilton arrived at Bletchley Park, he recalled:

> 'This man came over to speak to me and said, "My name is Alan Turing. Are you interested in chess?" And so I thought, "Now I am going to find out what it is all about!" So I said, "Well, I am, as a matter of fact." He said, "Oh, that is good because I have a chess problem here I can't solve."'

After this idiosyncratic introduction, Hilton got to know Turing well.

> 'Alan Turing was unique. What you realize when you get to know a genius well is that there is all the difference between a very intelligent person and a genius. With very intelligent people, you talk to them, they come out with an idea, and you say to yourself, if not to them, I could have had that idea. You never had that feeling with Turing at all. He constantly surprised you with the originality of his thinking. It was marvellous.'

Another colleague named Jack Good who worked with Turing did not rate him as a genius. 'Turing was a deep rather than a fast thinker,' he said, 'and therefore his IQ was not especially high.'

Others found him hard to work with. Senior cryptographer A. Dillwyn 'Dilly' Knox, a classics scholar and fellow of King's, complained:

'He is very difficult to anchor down. He is very clever but quite irresponsible and throws out a mass of suggestions of all degrees of merit. I have just, but only just, enough authority and ability to keep him and his ideas in some sort of order and discipline. But he is very nice about it all.'

He was once admonished for smuggling a barrel of cider into Hut 4 and was told in no uncertain terms to remove it. Due to wartime rationing, alcohol was in short supply.

ENIGMA SETTINGS PINCHED

Birch was unimpressed with their progress.

'I am worried about Naval Enigma,' he wrote in a memo. 'I've been worried for a long time, but I haven't liked to say as much . . . Turing and Twinn are like people waiting for a miracle, without believing in miracles.'

He went on to say: 'Hut 8 has not produced any results so far . . . Turing and Twinn are brilliant, but like many brilliant people, they are not practical. They are untidy, they lose things, they can't copy out right, and dither between theory and cribbing.'

But in March 1941, a miracle did happen. HMS *Somali* shelled the German trawler *Krebs* off the Lofoten Islands. Sheets giving the plugboard and rotor settings for the whole of February were found. The resulting decrypts gave the position of the weather ship *München* northeast of Iceland. The *Somali* pounced. This time its crew captured the plugboard and rotor settings for June. July's settings were pinched from the weather ship *Lauenburg* soon after.

In the North Atlantic, the U-boats were still taking their toll. On 9 May, *U-110* torpedoed SS *Bengore Head* and SS *Esmond* within seconds of each other. However, the Royal Navy corvette *Aubretia* got a sonar fix on her and dropped ten depth charges. When she was forced to the surface, a boarding party from HMS *Bulldog* found an Enigma machine, plugged in as if it had been in use when it was abandoned, and code tables. But Turing had already laboriously reconstructed these from the material pinched earlier. Nevertheless, the pinched code tables were a confirmation of his work.

By June 1941, the British were decoding the messages almost as quickly as the Germans. This was a godsend. Churchill's planners had predicted that the U-boats would have torpedoed Britain into starvation that June. Now the intelligence gleaned from the decrypts, known as Ultra, was used to steer the convoys away from the wolf packs. Churchill said later: 'The only thing that ever really frightened me during the war was the U-boat peril.' Now the U-boats in the North Atlantic went for twenty-three straight days without sighting a convoy. There was a danger, of course, that the Germans would realize that the Enigma code had been broken, so a rumour was circulated that the British had developed a new long-range radar that could detect submarines hundreds of miles away even when they were under the surface. And in 1942, when five Italian ships bound for Africa were sunk due to Ultra information, Churchill sent a telegram to Naples congratulating a fictitious spy and awarding him a bonus.

'It was thanks to Ultra,' Churchill told King George VI, 'that we won the war.'

RECOGNITION FROM ON HIGH

In July, Turing, Welchman and Alexander, who would take over from Turing in Hut 8, were called to Whitehall to be congratulated and given a bonus of £200. The following month, Turing took a short holiday, hill-walking with Joan Clarke in North Wales with their bicycles and ration books. Soon after they broke off their engagement.

Hugh Alexander wrote later:

'There should be no question in anyone's mind that Turing's work was the biggest factor in Hut 8's success. In the early days, he was the only cryptographer who thought the problem worth tackling and not only was he primarily responsible for the main theoretical work within the hut (particularly the developing of a satisfactory scoring technique for dealing with Banburismus) but he also shared with Welchman and Keen the chief credit for the invention of the bombe . . . the pioneer work always tends to be forgotten when experience and routine later make everything seem easy and many of us in Hut 8 felt that the magnitude of Turing's contribution was never fully realized by the outside world.'

ANOTHER CODE BOOK FOUND

While Britain and her Empire had stood alone in 1940, Hitler had turned against the Soviet Union in June 1941. Then after the attack on Pearl Harbor in December 1941 the United States had entered the war. Following Turing's letter to Churchill, Bletchley Park had obtained the recruits it needed. They were busily decoding German messages intercepted in North Africa, which helped Britain win its first victory in the war at El-Alamein, Egypt (23 October–4 November 1942).

Things were not going so well in Hut 8 though. In February 1942 the Kriegsmarine added a fourth rotor to the machine itself. Their cryptography department had built a reflector that was only half as wide as before. There were two different versions of this with different wiring and the narrower reflector left room for a new thin rotor. There were two versions of this too. As they were not interchangeable with the existing rotors, they were called beta and gamma. Again German navy intercepts went dark and Hut 8 had to await a fresh pinch.

In October, HMS *Petard* intercepted *U-559* in the eastern

BOMBE

A US navy 'bombe' decryption machine, which was based on a design by Turing

Mediterranean. Two of the boarding party were drowned when the submarine suddenly sank. But by then they had handed up the settings for October and November and a new code book. Soon Hut 8 was back in business.

Turing was bored by routine work and as far as he was concerned he had solved all the fundamental problems of cracking the naval Enigma.

TURING IN THE US

With America now in the war, United States cryptographers visited Bletchley Park, bringing with them a 'Purple' machine that they used to crack the Japanese codes. British and American codebreakers got on famously, but the atmosphere soured when the British refused to hand over a bombe. They were happy to part with detailed documents on the Enigma code and its cracking, including the detailed instructions Turing had provided, but at the time there were only six bombes and they were working day and night. Instead it was decided to send Turing himself.

In November 1942, he left for the United States to liaise with the cryptanalysts there. He sailed to New York on the *Queen Elizabeth*, the only civilian on a ship packed with military personnel. He must have hoped that Hut 8 was working overtime. More than a hundred Allied ships were sunk that month.

The operation at Bletchley Park was top secret and officially Turing was a low-level employee at the Foreign Office. United States immigration officers were reluctant to let him into America, but they eventually relented. His first port of call was Bell Labs in Manhattan, but he did not have the necessary security clearance. General George Marshall, Chief of Staff of the US army, said that Bell Labs housed work 'of so secret a nature that Dr Turing cannot be given access'. After a long correspondence between General Marshall and Churchill's personal representative in Washington DC, Turing was allowed into Bell Labs in January. Clearance had come from the White House itself. Bell Labs was then working on the encryption of speech and Bletchley Park wanted Turing involved. He was to help set up a secure line for speech across the Atlantic. On his first examination of the apparatus, he was not entirely satisfied with its security and suggested certain alterations.

Turing was a puzzle to his American colleagues. After being introduced as 'the top cryptoanalyst in England', he asked Alex Fowler to help him with a newspaper cryptogram from the *Herald Tribune*.

'I've never been able to do those,' said Turing.

Fowler had to upbraid Turing for never greeting colleagues or showing a hint of recognition as he passed them in the corridors. Instead, he seemed to look right through them. Turing explained: 'You know, at Cambridge, you come out in the morning and it's redundant to keep saying hallo, hallo, hallo.' However, he promised to try and do better.

Staying in a hotel in Greenwich Village, he was surprised by the casualness of a man who made a sexual approach. He gave no hint of this at Bell Labs, though he did once say: 'I've spent a considerable portion of time in your subway and I met someone who lived in your Brooklyn who wanted me to play Go.' On another occasion, he said:

'I had a dream last night. I dreamt I was walking up your Broadway carrying a flag, a Confederate flag. One of your bobbies came up to me and said, "See here! You can't do that," and I said, "Why not? I fought in the war between the states."'

His colleagues could not make him out, though he was revered for being the inventor of the Turing machine.

After two months, Turing travelled down to Washington to see the US navy codebreaking unit. He had already liaised with them when their cryptanalysts had visited Bletchley Park. He was allowed complete access there on the authority of the White House. He also visited Dayton, Ohio, where the National Cash Register Corporation was making bombes for the US navy. Turing was critical of the goings-on there and took a hand, but it was not until June 1943 that an American-made bombe broke an Enigma message. By the end of the year, however, Hut 8 gave Washington codebreakers the responsibility of decoding the Mediterranean traffic. This worked well because of the good transatlantic cable communications. By then there were so many bombes – two hundred by the end of the war – that they had to be accommodated in outstations, usually twenty or thirty miles from Bletchley Park.

Reports indicate that Turing had a hand in cracking the 'Hag' code used by the Italians, which was deciphered by a ten-foot-tall machine nicknamed 'Nightingale'. It was installed in an office above a ladies' dress shop in Mayfair. Turing also seems to have lent his expertise to breaking the Japanese JN-25 naval code, giving the United States victory at the Battle of the Coral Sea and the Battle of Midway.

97. 9 B A A 1 A . B O A   B 5 C 3
 82 8. 707F25 A 7 9 A2 DD F. 1 1A D9C0 A
 5A44   04B27A1C E 3BCDE 81E89B. 4549BCDC
   B82 9B8DBA89BA677D45FF8DF75A34AD
  7E0342ADC9672D8EE8F46FF90E63E2C061DC
 8AB90AA91DCE19EA87D45B82749 2C6 873 C8
  BA3087D38CBAB2B446FF0342AD9 91 AA1E8BA
 90472D8ADCCB3087D38AB245A6BA1B2B449ADA

The Birth of the Computer

42ADC1F25B430D9C00A6D8DF75A34F4129672D8EE
A91DC06E97BEA6A8E13F2E62E2C061ADCE19EA8
7D38C89EA8707F25BADAC62C6EC8789FCBAB2B
   6BA1B2B4490AA91D4789C9BAA1E3F021DADCC
 4F4161ADCCB3087D38AB27A8EE6137A1C389FCE03
   2BFB010FF7BA8C878906E97BCDEA8E3F0290
 CA2 0DF9 472 1E3 F89EA87D45FF38FD26D982
 7A1 6F 349 C C6 37 A1B2B446FF907256E80B10
 AB27A1C6EB33BCAB850CC89EA87D45FF7BA4AA0
  8DBA89BA675B430D9C0A1B2B446FF9047238
 4AA1C6B4. 0D9. 003F2E6D248F6D 8C89EE85EC
  7A B7B A6A 1 AC 2 FB O   BA1B 850C
 A 2 E.7 7 2   78 C 2   F .6 A D9

While Turing was away in the United States, he was still making a contribution to codebreaking. Before he left Bletchley Park he had been moved from Hut 8 into the Research Centre.

CRACKING THE TUNNY MACHINE

The Research Centre codebreakers were working on messages delivered by a new German Lorenz cipher machine, which produced coded traffic that the British cryptanalysts called 'Tunny'. Instead of encoding the message and then transmitting it by Morse code, which had to be decoded at the receiving end, the Tunny machine worked entirely automatically. The operator typed plain text in at one end and plain text was printed out on a teleprinter at the other. Developed in 1940, the first Tunny radio link began operating in June 1941.

A teleprinter used digital codes for each letter. The Tunny machine had twelve wheels that generated a stream of seemingly random numbers. These were added to the digital numbers when the message was sent. At the receiving end, the same numbers were subtracted again. All that was required was that the sending and receiving machines were set up in exactly the same way. The Germans were so confident in their new cipher machine that they transmitted the settings in clear text.

Military codebreaker Colonel John Tiltman realized that if you added two encrypted messages together, the random numbers generated by the Tunny machine would cancel out, leaving the two messages blended together. However, with a few intelligent guesses Tiltman found that it was possible to extract the two separate messages. Then a young man named Bill Tutte worked out exactly how the Tunny machine worked. They never tried to pinch one in case the Germans came up with something even more complicated.

But knowing how the machine worked and reading daily messages are two different things. This is where Turing came in. Using a pencil,

Cryptographers use modified British Typex cipher machines inside Hut 6 at Bletchley Park, c.1942

paper and a rubber, after a few weeks he delivered a method to crack the code. This was known as Turingery and Bletchley Park was soon reading top-secret messages signed by Hitler himself. During the Battle of Kursk in the summer of 1943 – the largest tank battle ever fought – decoded Tunny messages were sent to the Russians, telling them the deployment of every German division and unit. The Red Army won the battle decisively and advanced, almost unchecked, to Berlin.

On the way the Soviets captured Tunny machines, which they used after the war, seemingly unaware that the British could read their messages. The British also supplied Tunny machines to Idi Amin, dictator of Uganda in the 1970s, to keep tabs on what he was up to.

Turingery allowed codebreakers to work out the pin settings of the wheels in the Tunny machine, which were changed once in a while. Tutte then came up with a method that worked out the positions of the wheels at the beginning of every message. But there was a problem. It involved so much calculation that breaking just one message could take one person up to a hundred years. Max Newman, who had now joined the team at Bletchley Park, had seen electronic circuits counting radioactive emissions at Cambridge's Cavendish Laboratory and he suggested that Tutte's calculations could be done at high speed using an electronic calculator.

ROBINSONS VS. COLOSSUS

Turing had a new assistant, a telephone engineer named Tommy Flowers. During the Battle of Britain he had perfected the communication system that displayed the positions of German aircraft in Fighter Command's headquarters. After that he was sent to Bletchley Park, where he developed an electronic version of Turing's bombe using electric relays.

With the aid of Turing, Newman persuaded the head of code-breaking, Edward 'Jumbo' Travis, that an electronic machine was needed to break Tunny.

Turing introduced Flowers to Newman and Flowers took a look at Newman's prototype machine. This and its successors were called 'Robinsons' after the cartoonist William Heath Robinson, who drew excessively complex machines to perform absurdly simple tasks. It worked by passing paper tape very rapidly though an electronic counter. As it was mainly mechanical, largely using relays rather than electronic valves, Flowers decided that it would not provide the speed or reliability required. Indeed Robinsons were prone to catching fire. The paper tapes were always breaking and the counters were fairly unreliable and did not always give the same count.

Instead he proposed an entirely electronic machine using over one thousand thermionic valves, of the type found in radios. However, at the time this was thought to be impractical, because the heated filaments were apt to blow.

The reason for this, Flowers knew, was because a radio set was switched on and off, so the filament was regularly heating up and cooling down. If a valve was kept running all the time on a low current the filament rarely burnt out. As early as 1934, in his telephone work, he had successfully operated experimental equipment that used over three thousand valves.

Flowers describes the first stages of Colossus:

> 'I'd introduced valves into telephone equipment before the war and I knew that if you never moved them and never switched them off they would go on forever. They asked me how long it would take to produce the first machine. I said at least a year and they said that was terrible. They thought in a year the war would be over and Hitler could have won it so they didn't take up my idea. They decided they would proceed hopefully with the Robinson, which is what they did, and they left the question of whether the valve-based machine would be constructed or not to me.'

As a result, when the first Robinson was installed in Bletchley Park in June 1943 an ominous plume of smoke issued from its innards. It regularly broke down and in three months it decoded less than twenty intercepts.

Meanwhile back at the telephone labs in Dollis Hill, north London, in total secrecy, Flowers and his team set about building what would become the world's first full-function digital electronic computer.

Flowers went on:

> 'I was so convinced that Robinson would never work that we developed the new machine on our own at Dollis Hill. We made the first prototype in ten months, working day and night, six-and-a-half days a week, twelve hours a day sometimes. We started with the design of what was to be called Colossus in February 1943 and we had the first prototype machine working on 8 December.'

COLOSSUS DELIVERS THE GOODS

Delivered to Bletchley Park in January 1944, Colossus was the size of a room and weighed a ton. The input was from punched paper tapes strung around aluminium wheels supported on a frame called the bedstead. The tapes sometimes snapped, festooning the room. Output came from a manual typewriter with electromagnetically driven rods pressing the keys. Programming had to be done using switches and patch cables.

The purpose of Colossus was to find out what the positions of the Tunny machine code wheels were at the beginning of the message. It did this by trying all the possible combinations. There were billions of them. Processing at 5,000 characters a second, that task could be achieved in half an hour. But once you had the starting positions of the cipher wheels you could decode the message.

'It had about 1,500 valves in it, which horrified Bletchley Park,' said Flowers.

Immediately they put it to the test.

'What they did with Colossus, the first day they got it, was to put a problem on it to which they knew the answer. It took about half-an-hour to run. They let it run for four hours, repeating the process every half hour, and to their amazement, it gave the same answer every time. They really were amazed. It was reliable, extremely reliable'

– especially when compared to a Robinson.

Two weeks after it had arrived, Colossus cracked its first code. It was up and running ready for D-Day, giving the Allies crucial information about the Germans' plans. Ten were built. While early versions could read messages at 5,000 characters a second, later machines had five different input streams and could process 25,000 letters a second. This was comparable to the first Intel microprocessor chip introduced thirty years later.

'Colossus', the world's first electronic programmable computer, at Bletchley
Park in 1944

Although Newman had shown Flowers Turing's 1936 paper on
the Universal Machine, he did not understand much of it and had
not incorporated the all-important stored-program concept. Every
time Colossus was given a fresh set of instructions, the Wrens who
operated it had to rewire it by hand. It was not even an all-purpose
computer. Even long multiplication was beyond its scope. But when
it came to codebreaking, it did the job.

Though Turing has been given credit for Colossus, he had
nothing to do with its design. It was the work of Flowers. However,
its programming depended on key concepts developed by Turing
in Turingery and Banburism.

SIGSALY

When Turing returned from the United States in 1943, he got in
touch with Joan Clarke. Indeed he brought her back a present – an
expensive fountain pen – and dropped hints that they might resume

their relationship. These fell on deaf ears. Nevertheless, they remained friends.

He went to work in a small laboratory in a Nissen hut for the Secret Service's Radio Security Service at Hanslope Park, a few miles from Bletchley. At Bell Labs, the secure speech system he had been working on, SIGSALY, consisted of forty racks of equipment, weighing over fifty tons. One was installed in the Pentagon and a second was built in the basement of Selfridge's department store in London, so that Prime Minister Winston Churchill and President Franklin Roosevelt could have secure conversations day or night. At Hanslope Park, Turing went to work on a portable version, known as Delilah. It employed the same additive encoding system used by Tunny.

KEEPING A SECRET

At Hanslope, Turing lived in an old cottage and ate in the army mess. He was happy to give complicated lectures on mathematics, but what he said usually went over everyone's head. This did not make him unpopular. He was accepted as a wartime boffin with shiny trousers and unkempt hair who made strange noises when he worked. But he surprised everyone when he entered the mile race in the regimental sports and came first.

Turing made two close friends there, his assistant Don Bayley and Robin Gandy, who shared his hut and was working on improving intercept equipment. They were intrigued by the colleague who was so secretive about his previous contributions to the war. In May 1945, the three of them were out for a walk in the countryside together when Bayley said: 'Well, the war's over now, it's peacetime so you can tell us all.'

'Don't be so bloody silly,' said Turing. And that was the end of the conversation.

Everyone who had worked at Bletchley Park had signed the Official Secrets Act and were sworn to take its secrets to their grave until F.W.

Winterbotham, who had supervised the distribution of Ultra intelligence, published *The Ultra Secret* in 1974.

By then, it was too late for Turing to have his say.

In recognition of his work at Bletchley Park, Turing was awarded the Order of the British Empire in June 1945. He kept it in a box with nails and screws and other odds and ends.

Turing finally got Delilah working. He encoded one of Churchill's speeches – the enciphered version sounded like white noise. But with the war over, no one was interested in encryption any more. Besides, the Post Office were working on their own commercial scrambler.

POST-WAR TRIP TO GERMANY

After the war, Turing and Flowers travelled to Germany to examine the German cryptological systems. A talkative engineer showed them a Tunny machine, but they did not let on that they were already familiar with its workings.

Flowers recalled:

'This chap then explained how it worked and said didn't we think it was a marvellous machine and we all said yes. "But nevertheless," he told us in an incredulous voice, "our codes people said the enemy could break these messages after two years." I asked him if he had changed the machine after two years. "Oh no," he said. "Our factories were so disorganized by the bombing that we weren't able to make another machine. But it was safe, absolutely safe." That was quite a moment. It was a great temptation to turn to Turing and wink.'

The modifications the engineer had outlined would have put the codebreakers of Bletchley Park back to square one.

While Turing and Flowers were in Germany, news came that an atomic bomb had been dropped on Hiroshima. Flowers was surprised that Turing knew exactly how an atomic bomb worked. But after all, he was a scientist as well as a mathematician and it was his hero Einstein who had laid the theoretical groundwork for the atomic bomb.

They took a special interest in the Germans' codebreaking facilities. They had nothing on the scale of Bletchley Park. The German navy's B-Dienst (*Beobachtungsdienst* or Surveillance Service) had broken some Royal Navy ciphers, which kept the U-boats informed of the positions of convoys, but this was an isolated success. They thought it was unlikely that the Nazis could have run such an establishment as Station X, whose brightest intellects were often homosexuals or Jews.

TURING MACHINE BECOMES REALITY

By building Colossus, Flowers had shown Turing that it might be possible to build one of his Universal Machines. And Turing would soon be given the opportunity to do so. John Womersley, the head of the Mathematics Division at the National Physical Laboratory in Teddington, had read Turing's paper 'On Computable Numbers' soon after it had been published and began to draw up plans to make a Turing machine using equipment from an automatic telephone exchange. He then realized that the current machinery that used electromagnetic relays would be too slow to be effective. At that point the war intervened.

As the war drew to a close, he was discussing the matter with British physicist Douglas Hartree, who knew of Colossus but could say nothing. He suggested that, using electronics, he could make 'Turing in hardware'. Womersley then thought that it would be a good idea to employ the man himself. At the time, Turing's where-abouts were themselves a secret. But after the war was over, Max Newman put them in touch.

Due to his work on Delilah, Turing was now au fait with electronics and Womersley offered him the opportunity to build the first all-purpose electronic computer at the NPL. He was much in demand

at the time. When GC&CS became GCHQ in 1946, Hugh
Alexander, who had worked alongside Turing at Bletchley Park, offered
him £5,000 a year to break post-war codes, more than six times his
starting salary at the NPL. Turing refused and told Bayley he was
going to the NPL to 'make a brain'.

ACE BEATS OFF RIVAL EDVAC

Though Womersley knew nothing about Colossus he did know about
ENIAC (Electronic Numerical Integrator and Computer), which was
being built in Pennsylvania to calculate artillery firing tables. Von
Neumann had used it to test the feasibility of building a hydrogen
bomb. When it was unveiled to the public in 1946, he said it was
'the first electronic computing machine'. He, too, knew nothing of
Colossus. Although ENIAC was said to be 'Turing complete', it did
not have a storable program either. Like Colossus it was programmed
with switches and rerouting cables. Programming it and debugging
the program could take up to three weeks. However, the publicity
surrounding it gave Womersley the opportunity to convince the NPL's
director, Sir Charles Darwin, grandson of the author of *The Origin
of Species*, to let him design and build what he called the Automatic
Computing Engine (ACE).

Turing set about drawing up detailed designs for what he hoped
would be the first stored-program electronic computer. His proposal
for what he called an 'electronic calculator' ran to forty-eight pages
with fifty-two diagrams. The machine's memory would be around
the size of an early Apple Macintosh, with a clock speed of 1MHz.
Modern microprocessors run over a thousand times faster. It would
cost £11,200 – that's over £400,000 at today's prices.

Turing and Womersley were summoned to the offices of the Royal
Society in Piccadilly to explain the project to the NPL's executive
committee. The British government then agreed to fund the project,
promising £100,000 over three years.

In America, von Neumann, now consultant to the ENIAC project, realized that it was missing one vital element – Turing's stored program. It was the one thing that made Turing's machine 'universal'.

With the designers of ENIAC, John Mauchly and J. Presper Eckert of the University of Pennsylvania, he set about drawing up a proposal for a stored-program device called EDVAC (Electronic Discrete Variable Arithmetic Computer). Mauchly and Eckert's names were left off the paper and to the uninitiated it appeared that the stored-program idea was von Neumann's, who was heralded as the 'father of the computer'.

However, Mauchly and Eckert took umbrage and the EDVAC project faltered. They quit to form a computer company in Philadelphia, while von Neumann tried to set up a computer group in Princeton. Others finally built EDVAC, but it did not run its first program until 1952. By then it had been overtaken by other developments.

Even in 1946 ACE was well ahead of EDVAC. While von Neumann's theoretical proposal hardly mentioned the electronics, Turing had given detailed specifications of the hardware, along with sample programs in machine code. Nevertheless Turing did borrow from von Neumann's paper, but gave the Americans due credit. He had a different approach to computer design though. Instead of building hardware to deal with specific problems, he believed in keeping it to a minimum. Problems, he thought, should be dealt with by the software. After all, he had been writing complex computer programs since 1936. His approach made good sense at a time when the use of thermionic valves made the hardware intrinsically unreliable and he roundly condemned 'the American tradition of solving one's difficulties by means of much equipment rather than thought'.

The problem was that Turing did not get on with Womersley. Although Womersley was a mathematician with a considerable track record, Turing looked down on him. Among his team Turing offered a prize for the first person to spot Womersley using an equation. According to Robin Gandy: 'The competition was closed after three months for lack of entries.' Turing called Womersley 'Wormsley' –

emphasizing the 'worm'. Others accused Womersley of taking the credit that rightfully belonged to Turing. In fact it was Womersley who had given Turing the chance to make his dream a reality, but the bad blood between Turing and Womersley put the whole ACE project in jeopardy.

MARATHON MAN

There were other distractions. At the beginning of the war, Turing feared that a German invasion would provoke financial chaos, so he had sunk his meagre savings into silver. He bought two ingots. Carrying the heavy bars in a pram, he buried them in the countryside. When he went back after the war, he failed to find them, even with the aid of a home-made metal detector.

According to Peter Twinn his old assistant at Bletchley Park:

'He had all kind of crackpot notions based on the fact that he didn't think the currency would stand up to a substantial war. He wanted to keep something of value and he put a lot of money into silver bars. Having extracted them from his bank with the utmost difficulty, he went and buried them somewhere. He had a very elaborate set of instructions of how to find them after the war. But he never did find them. What he'd neglected to think about was that someone might build a new town like Milton Keynes over the site.'

Turing still travelled around on the ancient bicycle he had used throughout the war. Every so often the chain would come off. Rather than repair it, he would count the rotation of the pedals, jump off and walk a few paces, then remount. This prevented the chain coming off the sprocket. The procedure had been going on for five years. Even so, he went on cycling tours of France and Switzerland, even tackling the Alps.

Turing was now in training to run marathons and became a committee member of nearby Walton Athletic Club. When he needed to visit Flowers' lab in Dollis Hill, fifteen miles from the NPL, he would run there in old trousers. They were held up by a piece of rope with a clock hung from it, so he could time himself. He also ran the eighteen miles to his mother's house in Guildford for lunch. His athletic achievements on the sports field made the newspapers. A problem with his hip ruled him out of the 1948 London Olympics, but he remained a dedicated runner for the rest of his life.

TURING QUITS ACE PROJECT

Flowers believed that he could have a basic ACE up and running by the middle of 1946, but he was soon overworked in his principal occupation, repairing Britain's war-ravaged telephone system. Though the building of ACE fell behind schedule, Turing occupied his time writing programs for the non-existent machine.

One of the major problems was building the memory. ENIAC had used five hundred expensive glass valves to store a single ten-digit number. Turing toyed with the idea of using a 'delay line' originally developed for use with radar. This was a five-foot-long pipe, used to channel beeps of sound. Turing told the NPL that using this method he could store '1,000 binary digits at a cost of a few pounds'. He improved the performance of the device by filling the pipe with mercury to retard the sound waves travelling along it. When the beep reached the far end, it was converted back into an electric pulse, amplified and fed back into the beginning of the pipe again. The pulse would go round and round this circuit ad infinitum, thereby making a primitive memory.

There were problems though. The device had to be screened from electrical interference and the sound of passing traffic, and it had to be kept at a constant temperature. But by the spring of 1947, the mercury-line memory was working.

With Flowers unable to help, the NPL were going to have to build ACE themselves. Harry Huskey, an American who had previously worked on ENIAC, came to Britain to take charge. But he soon fell out with Turing. Turing was wedded to building ACE exactly as he had designed it, even though the NPL did not have the engineers who could do it. Huskey wanted to get the ball rolling by building a smaller computer that he called the Test Assembly. While Huskey got on with it, Turing simply ignored him.

At Turing's behest, the NPL finally set up a dedicated electronics group to build ACE. Its head, Horace Augustus Thomas, would brook no rivals. He demanded that the Test Assembly be shut down. When it was, Huskey quit and went back to the United States. Thomas then left. Turing took a sabbatical and returned to Cambridge, and the whole project to build ACE collapsed.

At Cambridge he did not even bother to look in on Maurice Wilkes, who was building a computer there. Wilkes, he said, looked like a beetle and was following in the footsteps of the Americans, seeking to solve problems with hardware while Turing thought they should be tackled with software.

When Turing visited the NPL for its sports day the following spring, winning the three-mile race, ACE was no further forward. Turing formally quit and accepted a post with Newman at the Computing Machine Laboratory at Manchester University, where Newman kept what was left of Colossus. He had arranged for the machine to be dismantled and taken to Manchester after all trace of its original purpose had been expunged.

ACE GOES AHEAD WITHOUT TURING

Soon after Turing quit the NPL, the Test Assembly was revived as the Pilot Model ACE, which ran its first program on 10 May 1950. Although a number of other computers were working by then, Turing's 1MHz processor meant that it far out-performed them. He had left behind a sheaf of programs and ACE was soon ready to tout for work from government departments.

English Electric made a commercial version of the Pilot Model ACE, called the DEUCE (Digital Electronic Universal Computing Engine), which was very successful. Thirty-three were sold, along with

The Pilot Model ACE, built at the National Physical Laboratory in Middlesex in 1950 and based on Turing's designs for the ACE computer

over a thousand programs and subroutines. The ACE itself was eventually completed as MOSAIC, the top-secret computer that ran Britain's air defences during the Cold War. Other commercial companies made their own versions of ACE and the NPL used Turing's design as the basis of their first supercomputer. Turing's philosophy of solving problems using software rather than hardware also endured along with his high clock speed, resulting in the modern personal computer.

BABY IS BORN

Meanwhile, Newman's chief engineer Freddie Williams had developed a new high-speed memory using cathode-ray tubes. Due to the introduction of television, these could be bought cheaply off the shelf. Data was stored digitally as lines of dots and dashes on a TV screen, so the computer did not have to wait for the bit it needed to reach the end of a mercury-filled tube. In fact, Turing had suggested this in his proposal at the NPL, months before Williams had become involved in the project, but Williams' wartime experience in radar gave him the expertise to make it happen and it was he who patented it. Von Neumann would go on to use Williams' memory tubes in Princeton.

Williams and his assistant Tom Kilburn, who had also worked in radar, had received their first grounding in computing at a course of lectures given by Turing in London in December 1946. Consequently, the computer they were designing in Manchester – 'Baby' – was built along Turing lines. But Newman had spent the winter of 1946 in Princeton with von Neumann, so Williams and Kilburn had to drop Turing's idea of a decentralized computer and incorporate von Neumann's idea of a CPU, or central processing unit.

On 21 June 1948, Baby became the first computer to run a stored program. True the program was just seventeen instructions long and it had to be programmed by hand. But Manchester had won the race. The Manchester company Ferranti then took Baby's design and produced the Ferranti Mark 1. This was delivered to Manchester University in February 1951. It was the first commercially available general-purpose electronic computer, beating Eckert–Mauchly's UNIVAC I (Universal Automatic Computer I) by over a month.

When Turing arrived in Manchester, Baby had no input or output devices. Switches inserted bits into the memory one at a time and the results appeared as a pattern of dots on a screen. He set about remedying that, while at the same time writing the world's first programming manual.

His input device was a tape reader that used light-sensitive cells to convert holes punched into the tape into electrical pulses. Although Colossus had used a similar device, this was twenty-five times faster. But when it came to engineering Alan Turing was no Tommy Flowers.

Turing did not get on with Kilburn, whom he described merely as 'the mechanic who constructed the machine'. Kilburn responded by restricting Turing's access to Baby to two nights a week. Alone throughout the night – which suited him – Turing renewed his interest in biology and began working on what he called 'artificial life' – that is, he devised programs that mimicked the way living things grow.

E97. 9 B A A   1 A . B . O . A   B 5 C 3
  82 8   707F25 A 7 9 A2 DD F. 1 1A D9C0 A
  5A446   04B27A1C E 3BCDE 81E89B. 4549BCDC
    B827 9B8DBA89BA677D45FF8DF75A34AD
   7E0342ADC9672D8EE8F46FF90E62E2C061DC
8AB90AA91DCE19EA87D45B8274962C6 C8739C8
  BA3087D38CBAB2B446FF0342AD9C9 BAA1E8BA1
90472D8ADCCB3087D38AB245A6BA1B2B449ADA

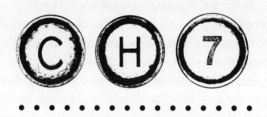

Men and
Machines

42ADC1F25B430D9C00A6D8DF75A34F4129672D8EE
A91DC06E97BEA6A8E13F2E62E2C061ADCE19EA8
7D38C89EA8707F25BADAC62C6EC8789FCBAB2B
  6BA1B2B4490AA91D4789C9BAA1E3F021DADCC
4F4161ADCCB3087D38AB27A8EE6137A1C389FCE03
2BFB010FF7BA8C878906E97BCDEA8E3F0290
CA2 DDF90472 1E3 F89EA87D45FF38FD26D982
7A1 6E 349 C 61 7A1B2B446FF907256E80B10
AB27A1C6EB33BCAB850CC89EA87D45FF7BA4AA0
  8DBA89BA675B430D9C0A1B2B446FF9047238
4AA1C6B4. 0D9. 003F2E6D248F6D 8C89EE85EC
  7A B7B A6A 1 AC 2 FB 0 BA1B 850C
A.2 E.772. 78 C 2   F .6 A D9

In 1951, Turing was elected a Fellow of the Royal Society. Two years later, Manchester University created a readership in computing especially for him. He moved out of his rented digs into a semi-detached house called Hollymeade in the suburb of Wilmslow. This gave him a ten-mile run or cycle ride from home to the university. Later, he added a motor to one of the wheels of his bike.

SEMI-DETACHED SUBURBAN TURING

It seems he was happy in his new home. He became friendly with the neighbours, had friends to stay, and a housekeeper, Mrs Clayton, came in to clean and cook for him. He visited Newman, who lived nearby in Bowden. Newman's wife Lyn would try and get him interested in the arts and literature. For the most part this was a failure, though she did get Turing to read Tolstoy's *War and Peace*.

Lyn Newman said Turing had an 'oddly shaped head' and a chin 'like a ship's prow'. He was 'handsome and even imposing', but he 'never looked right in his clothes. An alchemist's robe, or chain mail would have suited him . . . The chain mail would have gone with his eyes too, blue to the brightness and richness of stained glass.' But, she said, he had a strange way of not meeting your eyes and then sidling out of the door with a brusque and offhand word of thanks. However, when you did eventually establish eye contact, he demonstrated 'candour and comprehension . . . something so civilized that one hardly dared to breathe'. She said that once Turing had looked 'directly and earnestly at his companion, in the confidence of friendly talk, his eyes could never again be missed'.

Turing was quite open with Lyn. He was, she said, a 'guileless homo'. While they chatted, Max would play the piano. At Princeton, Newman would play duets with Einstein.

But while Turing was by no stretch of the imagination a musician, it was he who made a lasting contribution to music. While others

Turing was an excellent marathon runner – his best time of 2 hours, 46 minutes and 3 seconds was only 12 minutes slower than the winner of the men's marathon at the 1948 Olympics

simply considered the computer a high-speed calculating machine, Turing was still wedded to the idea of the Universal Machine. Seeing that the engineers had added a speaker to the Manchester computer as a warning device, Turing wrote a program that enabled it to emit musical notes.

Turing would run the twelve miles from his home to the Newmans' house, turning up at odd hours. Their son William recalled opening the door to him in the middle of the night. Turing had wanted to invite the Newmans to dinner, but having no paper to write on he was trying to scrawl a message on a leaf with a stick, before posting it through the letterbox.

Turing also accompanied the Newmans on a holiday in Wales. Among a number of intellectual luminaries who dropped by was Bertrand Russell. Turing, Russell and Newman passed the time in erudite debate.

While Lyn maintained that Turing had no interest in poetry, he wrote a number of short verses. One ran:

Hyperboloids of wondrous Light
Rolling for aye through Space and Time
Harbour those Waves which somehow Might
Play out God's holy pantomime.

Another said simply: 'The Universe is the interior of the Light Cone of the Creation.' He signed this 'Arthur Stanley', perhaps as a reference to Arthur Stanley Eddington, the mathematician and astrophysicist who confirmed Einstein's general theory of relativity at the solar eclipse in 1919 and wrote verse himself.

ELECTRONIC MUSIC

Christopher Strachey, nephew of the Bloomsbury biographer Lytton Strachey, went to work at the Computing Machine Laboratory. Turing had known him at King's before the war. He had already been involved in programming ACE and when he arrived at Manchester Turing gave him his programming manual which, Strachey said, was 'famed in those days for its incomprehensibility'. Strachey was a pianist and had heard of Turing's note-production program. He returned with a program that ran to twenty pages – up until then the longest program had been half a page. The program played 'God Save the King'. Soon the BBC broadcasted a recording of the Ferranti Mark 1 playing Glenn Miller's 'In the Mood' and 'Baa Baa Black Sheep'. Turing then told *The Times* that he was aiming to program a computer so that it behaved like a brain. Strachey went on to write a program that randomly produced love letters signed M.U.C. – Manchester University Computer. More practically, Turing used the computer to deal with his correspondence, turning it into the first word processor.

Strachey had already written a program to play draughts, or checkers, on ACE, but at Manchester he played the first game in which the computer told the human player what to do. The computer then looked ahead and considered the consequences of any move it might make.

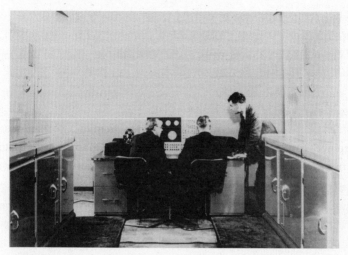

Turing and colleagues shown working on the Mark 1 at Manchester University in 1951

INTELLIGENT ROBOTS

Turing was already considering the possibility of a program that would learn like a child did. The machine would be like a pupil who 'learnt much from his master, but had added much more by his own work'. The key to building a computer that could think, Turing believed, was to 'provide the machine with the best sense organs that money can buy'.

As early as 1948, Turing envisaged a machine that would see by using television cameras, hear by using microphones, move on wheels, handle things using servo-mechanisms and communicate through loudspeakers. He proposed setting these robots free in the countryside, where they could learn without being distracted by 'food, sex, sport and many other things of interest to human beings'.

In 1973, Turing's friend and fellow codebreaker from Bletchley Park, Donald Michie, built just such a machine, called Freddy, though he did not let it roam the countryside. During the war he and Turing had conversed at length about machine intelligence and Turing had even circulated the typescript of a paper on the topic at Bletchley.

In his paper 'Proposed Electronic Calculator', written for the NPL, he mentioned that computers could 'probably be made to play very good chess'. He also anticipated the Internet in 1947, saying: 'It would be quite possible to control a distant computer by means of a telephone line.'

ARTIFICIAL INTELLIGENCE

In 1948, Turing and David Champernowne wrote the first artificial intelligence program. Called Turochamp, it was a chess-playing algorithm. It was a 'paper machine' because no electronic device that could execute it had been built at that time. Nevertheless, the program managed to beat Champernowne's wife. Later, Turing wanted to run it on the computer at Manchester, but Kilburn put his foot down. There is no record of Turing ever losing a game to an algorithm or a computer, though he did not rule such a thing out. This would have been a stringent test as by then Turing had spent years honing his chess-playing ability. He hung pictures of chessboard positions on his walls to improve his visualization and when out walking with a suitable opponent he could play without a chessboard, simply by calling out the moves and carrying the positions of the other pieces in his head.

When Turing wrote up the results of his year's sabbatical for Darwin, he called the resulting paper 'Intelligent Machinery'. Darwin dismissed it as a schoolboy essay. In fact Turing had introduced concepts vital to the development of artificial intelligence, including the generic algorithm which was later used in fields as diverse as financial forecasting and the design of drugs. The idea is to set two competing programs against each other. Small random changes are introduced. If these improve the performance of one of them, the other is discarded and the process is started again. Ironically, this is a Darwinian process – the survival of the fittest. In 1953, Turing tested it out with a chess-playing program.

Turing also introduced heuristics into chess programming. As the number of possible moves that could be made in a chess game is astronomically high, he realized that checking them all out would take an impossibly long time. So it was necessary to take short cuts by introducing rules of thumb. This is exactly what he had done with cribs and other short cuts when cracking the Enigma codes. Using approximations and rules of thumb, he realized, is an essential part of how we think.

According to Turing:

'Mathematical reasoning may be regarded rather schematically as the exercise of a combination of two faculties, which we may call intuition and ingenuity. Intuition consists of making spontaneous judgments which are not the result of conscious trains of reasoning. These judgments are often but by no means invariably correct (leaving aside the question what is meant by "correct").'

Turing believed that the role of ingenuity was 'aiding the intuition', not replacing it.

He was convinced that a computer could think. Once that happened, he warned: 'It would not take long to outstrip our feeble powers.'

In 1951, Turing told a radio audience: 'Even if we could keep the machines in a subservient position, for instance by turning off the power at strategic moments, we should, as a species, feel greatly humbled.'

TURING TEST

With Kilburn restricting his use of the computer, Turing spent more time theorizing. In an attempt to answer the question 'can automatic calculating machines be said to think?' he came up with the 'Turing test' or what he called the imitation game. This involves two humans and the machine being tested. The three are screened off so they cannot see each other. These days communication would be by screen and keyboard – Turing envisaged using a teleprinter link.

By asking a series of questions, one of the humans, the judge, must decide which of the other two is the machine. The human contestant does all they can to help the judge come to the right decision, the machine does everything in its power to fool the judge, who should not be an expert on machines. If asked 'are you a computer?' the machine will say no. Asked to work out a complicated bit of arithmetic, the machine will pause for a long time and come up with the wrong answer, but not so wrong that the judge will deduce that the contestant is a machine that is trying to fool them. To explain any awkwardness in its replies, the machine may claim that English is not its first language and it comes from Ukraine, for example.

The judges are changed once they have decided which is the human and which is the machine. If the rate at which they pick out the machine is no better than if they were guessing – one in two – then it has passed the Turing test and can be said to be intelligent. However, Turing pointed out that a machine that was genuinely thinking could also fail the test if its pattern of thought was distinctly alien. In 1952, Turing predicted that it would be a hundred years before any machine passed the test. In the meantime, a number of scientists and philosophers have come up with objections to the Turing test, but none have succeeded in overturning it.

Turing was also asked if he would say that a computer was conscious if it passed the Turing test. His reply was: 'I would say it was conscious or otherwise I would be punished.'

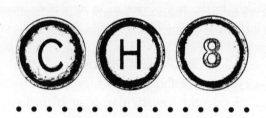

The Poisoned Apple

Turing was in his forties when he wrote a short story whose protagonist, Alec Pryce, was a has-been scientist who worked at Manchester. In his twenties he had made a discovery called 'Pryce's buoy'. An unrepentant homosexual, Pryce liked to pretend that the word was spelt without the 'u'. Like Turing, Pryce always wore 'an old sports coat and rather unpressed worsted trousers'. This undergraduate garb encouraged him to believe that he was still an attractive youth. In the story, Pryce picks up a male prostitute who is a petty thief. After taking him to lunch, they end up in bed.

FATAL ENCOUNTER

The short story was uncomfortably close to home. In December 1951, Turing met 19-year-old Arnold Murray in Manchester's Oxford Street, bought him lunch and then invited him over to his house in Wilmslow that weekend. Murray accepted the invitation but did not show up. However, Turing bumped into him again the following Monday afternoon. That time, Murray went home with him. Turing gave him a penknife as a Christmas present and they arranged to meet up again in January.

On 10 January Turing recorded a discussion at the BBC studios in Manchester with Sir Geoffrey Jefferson, professor of neurosurgery at Manchester University, Max Newman and philosopher Richard Braithwaite. It was about whether machines could think. Jefferson maintained that he would not believe that a computer could think until he saw it touch the leg of a lady computer, but this was cut out of the broadcast, which was aired on 14 January.

By then Murray had visited Turing's home again. They slept together and in the morning Murray stole some money from Turing's wallet. When he discovered the money was gone Turing wrote to Murray, saying that he did not want to see him again, but Murray turned up on his doorstep, protesting his innocence. Turing found himself half convinced by this display of indignation and when Murray asked to borrow some money Turing gave it to him, writing a cheque for £7.

A few days later Murray again asked to borrow money, on the pretext that he had bought a suit on hire-purchase and was behind on the payments. Turing asked for the name of the firm that Murray had dealt with – the truth of the matter was more important to him than the money. Murray was indignant over this seeming lack of trust.

A few days later, Turing returned home to find that his house had been burgled. A curious collection of items had been stolen, which Turing estimated were worth no more than £50 – £1,200 at today's prices. Turing reported the break-in to the police and two detectives came round to take fingerprints. He then wrote to Murray again. After mentioning the money that had gone missing from his wallet on the previous occasion, he said that it would be best if they stopped seeing each other. He then asked for the return of the money he had lent Murray.

Murray again came round to the house to protest his innocence and then threatened to go to the police and tell them everything. Homosexuality was against the law in Britain at the time. Turing thought this was an empty threat as Murray would have to incriminate himself, so he poured Murray a drink and tried to calm him down. Then he mentioned the break-in. Murray denied having anything to do with it, but said he thought he knew who had done it. He told Turing that he had been talking about him to a 21-year-old acquaintance named Harry, who had then suggested the robbery. Murray again insisted that he had taken no part in the crime.

RISKY STRATEGY

Turing's suspicions were allayed and they went to bed together. But in the middle of the night Turing began to have his doubts. He crept downstairs and hid the glass that bore Murray's fingerprints. The following morning, Murray waited outside the police station while Turing went inside to tell the detectives about Harry, the suspect, though he did not tell them how he had come by the information. This was a risky strategy, but Turing still had his suspicions about Murray and feared that not going to the police would be tantamount to giving in to blackmail.

The police knew all about Harry. He was already in custody on another charge and his fingerprints matched those in the house. When confronted, he told the police that Murray said he had 'business' at Turing's house. The two detectives went back to Hollymeade. They found Turing hard at work in an upstairs room filled with sheets of paper with strange mathematical symbols on them.

They told Turing that they 'knew all about it', not saying whether they meant the burglary or his affair. Then they asked him to repeat the description he had given of Harry. Turing said that he was about twenty-five years old and five feet ten inches tall. The police said they had reason to believe that the description was false and asked him why he was lying.

FULL CONFESSION

Turing then confessed everything, making none of the conventional excuses for his behaviour. After they cautioned him, he gave a statement – five handwritten pages – detailing everything that had taken place, though some of his phraseology was beyond them.

'He was a real convert . . . he really believed he was doing the right thing,' said one of the officers. They both concluded that he was 'a very honourable man'.

It was clear that Turing did not understand the seriousness of the offences he was admitting. He had lived his whole life in academia where homosexuality was commonplace. The only thing he said in mitigation was that he believed that a Royal Commission was sitting which would 'legalize it'. He was wrong. A committee under Lord Wolfenden looking into the laws concerning homosexuality and prostitution sat two years later in 1954. The Wolfenden report was published in 1957 and in 1967 the law was amended to legalize private homosexual acts between two men over the age of twenty-one. Having sex with 19-year-old Murray would not have been legal until the Criminal Justice and Public Order Act of 1994, which set the homosexual age of consent at eighteen. It was only the passage of the Sexual Offences (Amendment) Act in 2000 that equalized the age of consent for homosexual and heterosexual acts, making it sixteen in both cases.

Turing and Murray were charged with gross indecency under the Criminal Law Amendment Act of 1885, also known as the Labouchere Amendment, formerly used to prosecute Oscar Wilde. Turing admitted that they had indulged in sex on three occasions. There was the reciprocal crime of commissioning an act of gross indecency, so they were charged with six offences in all. At the committal proceedings, Turing's bank manager was called to give details of the £7 cheque. Turing was released on £50 bail, while Murray remained in custody.

The case was reported in the local newspaper, which also carried a photograph of Turing. He wrote to his brother, telling John: 'I suppose you know I am a homosexual.' John did not know this. He thought Alan was simply a misogynist. Alan said that he was going to plead not guilty, so John travelled to Manchester to see Alan's solicitor. They persuaded him to change his plea to guilty as he had already admitted the offences in a written confession. Otherwise, John showed little sympathy for his brother's plight.

Alan then had to tell their mother. This was a daunting task. When he had been at school, she had always sided with his teachers. This time she rallied to his defence.

Newman was shocked when Turing told him that he had been arrested, particularly because he announced the details in a loud voice in the university refectory so that everyone could overhear. But he and Hugh Alexander, now at GCHQ, both agreed to appear as character witnesses.

Young men at 'La Caverne' club in Soho in 1955. Until the passing of the Sexual Offences Act in 1967, homosexuality was illegal in the UK

Despite his legal problems, Turing did not stop working. He was developing mathematical theories to describe how biological entities develop and grow, he completed the revisions to a paper he had written on morphogenesis and he attended lectures and conferences.

STANDS TRIAL

The trial opened in the Cheshire town of Knutsford on 31 March 1952. Both Turing and Murray pleaded guilty on all twelve counts. However, the prosecution maintained that Turing's statement demonstrated that he felt no guilt or remorse. His only plea in mitigation was that he was otherwise of good character. Newman was asked whether he would receive such a man in his home. He replied that he and his wife had already done so. Not only was Turing 'particularly honest and truthful,' he said, 'he is completely absorbed in his work and is one of the most profound and original mathematical minds of his generation'.

His wartime codebreaking work could not be brought up. But his

OBE was mentioned and Hugh Alexander said he was a 'national asset'.

Turing's lawyer pointed out that:

'It would be a loss if a man of his ability – which is no ordinary ability – were not able to carry on with it. The public would lose the benefit of the research work he is doing. There is a treatment which could be given him. I ask you to think that the public interest would not be well served if this man is taken away from the very important work he is doing.'

But Murray's lawyer sought to thrust the blame on Turing. It was Murray who had been approached by Turing, not the other way round.

'He has not such tendencies as Turing,' he said, 'and if he had not met Turing he would not have indulged in that practice.'

CHEMICAL CASTRATION

Murray was conditionally discharged. On the same day, Harry was sent to Borstal for other offences. Turing, however, was sentenced to a year's probation on the condition that he 'submit for treatment by a duly qualified medical practitioner at Manchester Royal Infirmary'. He was to undergo what was known as 'chemical castration'.

'I am both bound over for a year and obliged to take this organo-therapy for the same period,' Turing wrote. 'It is supposed to reduce sexual urge whilst it goes on, but one is supposed to return to normal when it is over. I hope they are right.'

The treatment consisted of flooding his body with female hormones. As a result, he began to grow breasts. In a letter to another friend, he wrote: 'No doubt I shall emerge from this a different man, but quite who I've not found out.'

For Turing, going to prison for a year would not have been much of a problem. It would have been like being back at Sherborne. However, it would have cost him his job and access to computers.

MI5 TARGET

The Soviet spies Guy Burgess and Donald Maclean had fled to Moscow in 1951 and there were fears that a homosexual spy ring had been set up in Cambridge in the 1930s, when Turing was there. As a result, Turing was stripped of his security clearance and could no longer work for GCHQ. He was also being watched, so he had to be careful. MI5 and the SIS did not want to be caught napping again.

'If I had so much as parked my bicycle on the wrong side of the road there might have been twelve years for me,' he wrote.

In the summer of 1952, Turing took a holiday in Norway after being told that there were men-only dances there. On the trip, he met Kjell Carlsen.

'A very light kiss beneath a foreign flag, under the influence of drink, was all that ever occurred,' said Turing. Nevertheless, for Turing, it was an important act of defiance. But when Carlsen planned to visit him in the UK there were problems. Turing's mail was being monitored. The postcard announcing Carlsen's arrival was read and he was intercepted.

'At one stage police over the N of England were out searching for him, especially in Wilmslow, Manchester, Newcastle etc.' Turing wrote. 'He is back in Bergen now without my even seeing him.'

PSYCHOANALYTIC THERAPY

Despite what Turing called the 'Kjell crisis', he continued his work. The Royal Society published his paper outlining a new mathematical theory on how things grow and he was using the Manchester computer to simulate the chemical processes involved.

Now that higher-level computer languages were being developed, Turing began to work at home most of the time. He left most of his work on the machine to an assistant. While his interest in hands-on computing was waning, he became more interested in psychology, attending a series of lectures by Swiss psychologist, Jean Piaget, who connected symbolic logic with his observations of children's cognitive development. He also began seeing Jungian psychoanalyst Franz Greenbaum.

Despite his conviction, Turing felt no guilt about his homosexuality because in the 1950s homosexuality was widely seen as a sickness. One could hardly be blamed for being ill. Greenbaum himself did not take this view. However, he felt that he could offer Turing some psychological insight and got him to write down his dreams. These soon filled three notebooks. While his dreams seemed to indicate an antipathy towards his mother, since his trial they had become closer.

Turing's dedication to science was undiminished. When Francis Crick and James Watson discovered the molecular structure of DNA in March 1953, Turing followed up with his theory of 'reaction–diffusion', where complex wavefronts of chemicals flow through the embryo, stimulating the differential growth of structures within it.

He was also experimenting with chemical electrolysis in a laboratory he had built next to the bathroom at home. Mrs Turing called this the 'nightmare room', fearing there would be an accident. And he went back to Sherborne to give a talk on computers to the science society. Even so he complained of his tendency 'to fritter away time in anything but what I ought to be doing'.

Rather than being chastened by his conviction, Turing became more brazen. He regaled those who would listen with 'saga-ettes'. One concerned a young man he had picked up in Paris, who insisted on putting his trousers under the mattress to preserve the crease. He then persuaded Alan to swap watches to prove their mutual trust until they met again the following day. As a result, Turing lost his watch.

And when a handsome PhD student arrived from London to use the computer, Turing invited him to dinner, only to be fobbed off with a thin excuse about a sick aunt. According to Greenbaum, Turing was attracted to people like himself. Turing was intrigued by this insight, though it was commonplace, and wrote to Lyn Newman saying: 'Greenbaum has made great strides in the last few weeks. We seem to be getting near the root of the trouble now.'

Turing was invited to the Greenbaums socially from time to time. He played with Greenbaum's young daughter Maria, but did not get on well with Greenbaum's wife. When he raved about a youth in the next-door garden whom she did not find attractive, she complained he was 'obsessed with sex'.

SHOCK DEATH

Initially, the hormone had been administered to Turing as a pill, but after nine months an implant was put in his thigh. He had it taken out. After his period of probation was over, Manchester University created a new readership in the theory of computing for him and gave him a pay rise. The position was initially for ten years. During that time he would work as he chose. Life was on the up and he took a holiday in Corfu. So everyone was shocked when Alan Turing was found dead on Tuesday 8 June 1954.

The previous week, he had been working alongside computer engineer Owen Ephraim, who fixed the Manchester Mark 1. He was a busy man because one of its 100,000 components – usually one of its 20,000 valves – went wrong as often as every hour.

'Turing was quiet and focused on his work,' said Ephraim. 'We did not chat nor have any contact that was not related to the work in hand. He was seventeen years older than myself and I had no idea of his previous work.'

Ephraim had a junior named Frank whom he was supposed to train.

'On one occasion I found him in the computer room when I arrived on the Monday morning. He claimed to have spent the nights in a broom cupboard as he did not wish to travel home. I did not report his misdemeanour and it was not repeated. He

left abruptly soon after Easter as I remember and I now suspect
he was an MI5 plant to watch Turing.'

After their last shift together, Turing said 'cheerio' to Ephraim as
usual. Ephraim said he never suspected anything was wrong, even
when Turing did not turn up the following Tuesday morning, as he
was absent from time to time.

'I did not hear about his suicide until Thursday or Friday,' he said.

Neither the police nor the coroner asked him about Turing's behaviour
in those last days.

'If I had been asked, I would have said that Alan Turing acted
perfectly normally,' he said, 'and with as much dedication as ever.'

It was Turing's housekeeper Eliza Clayton who discovered the
body when she arrived at Hollymeade at around 5 pm on the 8th to
make his dinner. She had been away for a few days over the bank
holiday weekend. When she let herself in through the back door as
usual, there was no sign of Turing. Then she noticed that the light
was on in his bedroom. She knocked on the door and when there
was no reply she went in.

'I saw Turing lying in bed,' she said. 'He was on his back and
appeared to be dead. I touched his hand which was cold.'

She called the police from a neighbour's house. When Sergeant
Cottrell arrived, they returned to the bedroom where he examined
the body. Cottrell said Turing was dressed in his pyjamas with the
bedclothes pulled up around his neck. There was white foam around
his lips and a smell of bitter almonds, telltale signs of cyanide. His
wristwatch was on the bedside table, alongside an apple with a few
bites taken out of it. Apparently, it was Turing's habit to nibble on
an apple before he went to sleep.

The only unusual thing Mrs Clayton spotted was that he had left
his shoes outside the bedroom door. Cleaning his shoes was not one
of her duties.

It seems that Turing had died sometime during the night of

*Turing photographed with friends in his youth. Reflecting on his death, Turing's
mother insisted that her son 'had everything to live for'*

Monday 7 June, after eating mutton chops. The police pathologist
found that he had died of cyanide poisoning.

A vat of cyanide was found in the 'nightmare room' between his
bedroom and the bathroom. He had been using it to electroplate
cutlery. Turing was fond of making things at home. At Bletchley
Park, when someone stole his chess set, he made another from clay,
firing the chess pieces in a tin over an open fire. Robin Gandy had
come to stay at Hollymeade recently and Turing had told him of his
'desert island game' – making a range of chemicals from common
substances found around the home.

SUICIDE VERDICT

There was a rushed inquest just two days after the body was found.
The coroner ruled that Turing had committed suicide 'while the

balance of his mind was disturbed'. No evidence was given about the state of Turing's mind, but the coroner said: 'I am forced to the conclusion that this was a deliberate act. In a man of this kind, one never knows what his mental processes are going to do next.'

The verdict has been questioned ever since.

Turing's mother never accepted it. She believed that Alan had transferred cyanide to his hands while experimenting and had ingested it by accident. The previous Christmas, she had told him off for not washing his hands and then putting his fingers in his mouth. However, the apple on the bedside table was never tested for cyanide and it has never been established how he took it, or whether it was by design or accident.

'It is unlikely that Alan had any financial worries, since he had left a substantial credit at the bank,' his mother said. 'He was at the apex of his mental powers, with growing fame, and absorbed in his research on morphogenesis, which promised far-reaching results. By any ordinary standards he had everything to live for.'

Dr Greenbaum wrote to her saying: 'There is not the slightest doubt to me that Alan died by an accident.'

However, his daughter remembered that in mid May 1954 Turing had accompanied the family on a trip to Blackpool. There he had disappeared into the tent of the 'Gypsy Queen', a fortune-teller, while the family waited outside. When he came out, half an hour later, he was ashen-faced.

ACCIDENT OR MURDER?

Robin Gandy, who stayed with Turing on the weekend before he died, said that if anything Turing seemed happier than usual. Then on the Thursday before his death, he threw a tea party for the young son of a neighbour. The boy's mother found him perfectly cheerful.

'It was such a jolly party,' Mrs Clayton said.

It later transpired that Turing had made notes on what he planned to do the following week. He had also written a letter accepting a

Royal Society engagement later that month. The day his body was found he had an appointment with a postgraduate student, whose work confirmed Turing's theory of biological growth.

It is also unlikely that he was suffering from depression following his so-called chemical castration. Turing was said to have endured the hormone therapy with amazing fortitude. It had ended over a year before he died and he had recently returned from a holiday on Corfu, where he had enjoyed sun, sand and the company of men whom he described as 'luscious'.

At the time Don Bayley was puzzled.

'It's a complete mystery to me because he did enjoy life so much,' he wrote. However, he later confirmed that Turing was quite capable of putting his apple down in a pool of cyanide without noticing it. So he could easily have killed himself in a careless accident.

Another possibility was that Turing was killed by cyanide gas. The electroplating vat was connected to the mains and was bubbling when Sergeant Cottrell found it. He reported a strong smell of cyanide in the makeshift laboratory. The post-mortem found fluid in his wind-pipe and lungs that smelt of burnt almonds, but Turing might not have noticed it. When a toxic concentration of cyanide builds up in the system, the ability to smell it diminishes. There again, the pathologist smelt cyanide in his stomach, though he noted that this could be due to swallowing fluid from his respiratory system.

There is also the theory that Turing was murdered. There were indications that the Manchester computer was being used by the British government for the purposes of encryption. From the work of Bletchley Park, they knew that codes could be broken and were always looking for ways to update security. The Ferranti Mark 1 was also being used for atomic weapons research. Twelve days after Turing died, Julius and Ethel Rosenberg were executed in the United States for passing atomic secrets to the Soviet Union. British atomic spy Klaus Fuchs was already serving fourteen years in jail. Senator Joseph McCarthy's 'Red Scare' in the United States was at its height. The witch-hunt sought out homosexuals as well as suspected Communists, believing them to be security risks. It is certain that the British security services were taking a particular interest in Turing and former spy David Cornwell, aka author John le Carré, said they were known to carry out 'assassinations at arm's length'.

Turing left behind a great deal of unfinished work, including the material for a second paper on biological growth. He was working with Robin Gandy on mathematical 'type theory'; they planned to publish a joint paper. And his article 'Solvable and Unsolvable Problems' was published posthumously in *Science News* in 1954.

After seeing a double rainbow in May 1954, he set about analysing the phenomenon. He had also renewed his interest in theoretical physics and was working on a paradox he had found within the standard interpretation of quantum mechanics.

'Quantum mechanists always seem to require infinitely many dimensions,' he said. 'I don't think I can cope with so many – I'm going to have a hundred or so – that ought to be enough, don't you think?'

97. 9 B A A 1A. B .0 A   B 5 C 3
82 8. 707F25 A 7 9 A2 DD F. 1 1A D9C0 A
5A446   04B27A1C E 3BCDE 81E89B. 4549BCDC3
   B827 9B8DBA89BA677D45FF8DF75A34AD
 7E0342ADC9672D8EE8F46FF90E62E2C061DC
8AB90AA91DCE19EA87D45B827492C6 8873 C8
 BA3087D38CBAB2B446FF0342AD9 9 AA1E8B 1
90472D8ADCCB3087D3 AB245A6BA1B2B449ADA

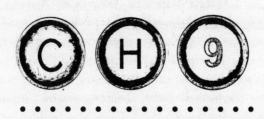

Turing's Legacy

42ADC1F25B430D9C00A6D8DF75A34F4129672D8EE8
A91DC06E97BEA6A8E13F2E62E2C061ADCE19EA8
7D38C89EA8707F25BADAC62C6EC8789FCBAB2B
 6BA1B2B4490AA91D4789C9BAA1E3F021DADCC
4F4161ADCCB3087D38AB27A8EE6137A1C389FCE034
 2BFB010FF7BA8C878906E97BCDEA8E3F0290
 CA2 0DF9 472 1E3 F89EA87D45FF38FD26D982
7 1 6 B 349 C C 613 A1B2B446FF907256E80B10
AB27A1C6EB33BCAB850CC89EA87D45FF7BA4AA0
 8DBA89BA675B430D9C0A1B2B446FF9047238
4AA1C6B4. 0D9. 003F2E6D248F6D 8C89EE85EC
 7A B7B A6A 1 AC 2 FB 0 BA1B 850C
A. 2 E. 7 7 2. 78 C 2   F .6 A D9

Alan Turing's body was cremated at Woking Crematorium on 12 June 1954. His ashes were scattered. There was no gravestone, plaque or memorial. The Royal Society published a biography the following year, but his work as a wartime codebreaker could still not be acknowledged. The only reference to it was: 'For his work at the Foreign Office he was awarded the OBE.'

LIFTING THE VEIL OF SECRECY

In 1966, America's Association for Computing Machinery established the annual A.M. Turing Award for technical innovation in the field of computing. At that point only Turing's post-war contribution to computing science with ACE and his work at the Manchester Computing Machine Laboratory was known about. But with the publication of Frederick Winterbotham's *The Ultra Secret* in 1974, the official ban on any mention of Ultra was lifted. The book caused a sensation, explaining how seemingly unbreakable German machine ciphers had been broken and revealing that the intelligence obtained had been circulated to Winston Churchill, President Roosevelt and all the principal chiefs of staff and commanders in the field throughout the war. It brought the Enigma code and Bletchley Park to the attention of the public in a big way.

Winterbotham made one reference to computers in his book:

'It is no longer secret that the backroom boys of Bletchley use the new science of electronics to help them . . . I am not of the computer age nor do I attempt to understand them, but early in 1940 I was ushered with great solemnity into the shrine where stood a bronze coloured face, like some Eastern Goddess, who was destined to become the oracle of Bletchley.'

But there was no mention of Alan Turing or any of the others who had helped build Bletchley Park's codebreaking machines.

The following year *Bodyguard of Lies: The Vital Role of Deceptive Strategy in World War II*, by Anthony Cave Brown, was published. It took its title from Winston Churchill's aphorism: 'In wartime, truth is so precious that she should always be attended by a bodyguard of lies.' This revealed more details about the Enigma machine and the Polish cryptanalysts who had first broken the code. It also mentioned Alan Turing and the codebreaking 'bombe' at Bletchley Park. But it made no mention of computers and referred to electronics only in connection with radio and radar.

Brian Randell, professor of computing science at the University of Newcastle upon Tyne, was intrigued. He had already petitioned the government to declassify information about the Colossus project. This had been refused and his request had caused ructions on both sides of the Atlantic. But it seemed to him that there had now been significant changes to government policy. He was summoned to the Cabinet Office in London, where he was shown photographs of Colossus and an explanatory paper.

RANDELL'S COLOSSUS PAPER

Randell was given permission to interview people involved in the project, but only after they had been briefed, and material was made available at the Public Record Office (now the National Archives) with a view to him writing a history of Colossus. This, however, would have to be submitted for approval before publication. He agreed.

Four months later, Randell could write to Alan's mother, telling her that 'the government have recently made an official release of information which contains an explicit recognition of the importance of your son's work to the development of the modern computer'.

He interviewed the designers of Colossus, including Max Newman, Tommy Flowers, his assistant Sidney Broadhurst, Post Office engineer Bill Chandler, classics scholar and cryptanalyst Donald Michie and a handful of others. Other interviews were tape recorded in America and Randell corresponded with his sources. Over thirty years memories had dimmed and it was important to get the chronology right.

But Flowers was emphatic. In one letter he said:

> 'In our wartime association, Turing and others provided the requirements for machines that were top secret and have never been declassified. What I can say about them is that they were electronic (which at that time was unique and anticipated the ENIAC), with electromechanical input and output. They were digital machines with wired programs. Wires on tags were used for semi-permanent memories, and thermionic valve bi-stable circuits for temporary memory. For one purpose we did in fact provide for variable programming by means of lever keys which controlled gates which could be connected in series and parallel as required, but of course the scope of the programming was very limited. The value of the work I am sure to engineers like myself and possibly mathematicians like Alan Turing was that we acquired a new understanding of and familiarity with logical switching and processing because of the enhanced possibilities brought about by electronic technologies which we ourselves developed. Thus when stored-program computers became known to us we were able to go right ahead with their development. It was lack of funds which finally stopped us, not lack of know-how.'

The paper was submitted on 12 April 1976 and some minor changes had to be made. Randell was not allowed to make any explicit reference to codebreaking – what the machine was for. All he was allowed to say was:

> 'The nature of the work that was undertaken at Bletchley Park during World War II is still officially secret but statements have

been appearing in published works in recent years which strongly
suggest that it included an important part of the British government's cryptological effort.'

As he was also allowed to leave in references to *The Ultra Secret* and
Bodyguard of Lies, it was clear what Turing and his colleagues had
been up to.

Of Turing himself, Randell said:

'Turing, clearly, was viewed with considerable awe by most
of his colleagues at Bletchley because of his evident intellect
and the great originality and importance of his contributions,
and by many with considerable discomfort because his
personality was so outlandish. Many people found him incom-
prehensible, perhaps being intimidated by his reputation but
more likely being put off by his character and mannerisms.
But all of the Post Office engineers who worked with him
say that they found him very easy to understand – Broadhurst
characterized him as "a born teacher – he could put any
obscure point very well". Their respect for him was immense,
though as Chandler said "the least said about him as an
engineer the better".'

This point is echoed by Michie who said 'he was intrigued by devices
of every kind, whether abstract or concrete – his friends thought it
would be better if he kept to the abstract devices but that didn't deter
him'.

JAWS DROP AT LOS ALAMOS

Once the paper was cleared, Randell submitted it to the International
Conference on the History of Computing to be held in Los Alamos
in June 1976. He was to be accompanied by Dr A.W.M. 'Doc'
Coombs, who took over work on the Colossus project when Flowers

moved on to other things and handled the day-to-day running of the machine.

Computer scientist Bob Bemer, sometimes known as the 'father of ASCII', also attended the conference, along with Dr John Mauchly, of ENIAC and UNIVAC fame, and Professor Konrad Zuse, who had already delivered a paper about his use of relay computers to trim the control surfaces on the V-1 buzz bombs fired at London during the war. He said that Hitler had refused to allow him to develop an electronic computer for Germany, saying it would not be needed because the V-2 rockets were going to be so successful.

The night before Randell's paper was going to be delivered, Bemer attended a reception given by the Director of the Los Alamos Labs in the Red Room of the Ray Bradbury Science Museum, where he met Dr Coombs, who was 'so excited about something that he was literally bouncing up and down'. Bemer asked him the cause of his excitement. Coombs replied: 'You'll know tomorrow morning – you'll know.'

The following day Professor Randell came on stage and asked if anyone had ever wondered what Alan Turing had done during the Second World War. He then showed slides of a place called Bletchley Park.

'After a while he showed us a slide of a lune-shaped aperture device he had found in a drawer whilst rummaging around there,' said Bemer. 'Turned out it was part of a 5,000-character-per-second paper tape reader.'

Bemer was astounded.

'From there he went on to tell the story of Colossus, the world's really first electronic computer, used to break the German Enigma cipher. Of course everyone knows about it now. Much has been written on the subject. And most have agreed that the Allies could very well have lost the war without the services of Colossus and its successors in unbuttoning Enigma. But that

day at Los Alamos was close to the first time the British Official
Secrets Act had permitted any disclosures.'

Bemer kept an eye on the reactions of those around him.

'I looked at Mauchly, who had thought up until that moment
that he was involved in inventing the world's first electronic
computer. I have heard the expression many times about jaws
dropping, but I had really never seen it happen before. And
Zuse – with a facial expression that could have been anguish.
I'll never know whether it was national, in that Germany lost
the war in part because he was not permitted to build his
electronic computer, or if it was professional, in that he could
have taken first honours in the design of the world's most
marvellous tool.'

He understood then why Coombs was so excited.

'Just imagine the relief of a man who, a third of a century later,
could at last answer his children on "What did you do in the war,
Daddy?"'

BBC PROGRAMME REVEALS ALL

Randell's paper, along with the Colossus photographs, was circulated
and published in *New Scientist* in February 1977. By then he had been
approached by the BBC, who were running a series called *The Secret
War*. The last episode – *Still Secret* – was going to be about Enigma.
While Randell had needed to be guarded about what he said, this
blew the wraps off the participation of Turing and the development
of the bombe and Colossus. When the programme aired, the wartime
contribution of Alan Turing was fully in the public domain.

But Turing's activities at Bletchley Park had been even more vital
than many realized. When Professor Harry Hinsley, a veteran of
Bletchley Park and senior author of the multi-volume official history

British Intelligence in the Second World War, gave a lecture at Newcastle University, Randell asked him: 'If this work was so effective, why didn't it shorten the war?'

Hinsley's reply was short and to the point: 'It did, by about two years.'

SAVING BLETCHLEY PARK

At the end of the war, most of the documents and much of the equipment at Bletchley Park had been destroyed. The Government Code and Cypher School became the Government Communications Headquarters (GCHQ) in June 1946 and moved first to RAF Eastcote in west London and then to Cheltenham, where it now occupies the famous 'Doughnut' building. Secrecy is not what it used to be.

Bletchley Park was handed over to the government-run General Post Office as a training centre for telephone engineers. GCHQ also used it as a training centre and British Telecom set up a management school there. It was later used as a teacher training college and housed the Property Advisers to the Civil Estate, a branch of the civil service.

By 1990, the place was deserted and buildings began to crumble. In the main house, the ceilings were coming down and the huts where the codebreaking had been carried out were derelict. The government was in no hurry to do anything about it as they did not actually own the estate. It had been bought privately in 1937 by the head of the Secret Intelligence Service, the late Admiral Hugh Sinclair, when Whitehall was dragging its feet over finding a new home for the codebreakers.

Veterans of Bletchley Park decided that something must be done to preserve such an important site. Tommy Flowers' laboratories in Dollis Hill, where the first Colossus was built, had already been sold off and converted into upmarket apartments. So in 1991, the Bletchley Park Trust was established. It raised money to restore the buildings and Bletchley Park was opened as a museum.

Before a major restoration project began in 2012, many of the huts at Bletchley Park lay abandoned

In 2005, a donation by American millionaire Sidney Field paid for the construction of a new science centre dedicated to Alan Turing. Three years later, a letter to *The Times* condemned the derelict state of Bletchley Park. A renewed fund-raising campaign and money from the National Lottery allowed the Trust to complete the restoration of the site. Bletchley Park is also home to the National Museum of Computing, which houses a working replica of Colossus and in Block B there is a rebuilt bombe.

TRIBUTES AND PORTRAYALS

British mathematician and gay activist Andrew Hodges produced the 600-page biography *Alan Turing* in 1983, detailing Turing's key role in breaking the Enigma code. Three years later, the play *Breaking the Code* by Hugh Whitemore opened in London's West End, starring Derek Jacobi as Turing. The following year it transferred to Broadway with Jenny Agutter playing Pat Green, a character based on Joan Clarke, where it was nominated for three Tony awards. The play was adapted for television by the BBC in 1996, airing in the United States on PBS. It was nominated for two BAFTAs and won Britain's

Broadcasting Press Guild award. There were also German and Italian productions of the play.

In 1998, English Heritage unveiled a blue plaque outside Turing's birthplace in Warrington Crescent, Maida Vale. A second blue plaque appeared on his home in Wilmslow on 7 June 2004, marking the fiftieth anniversary of his death. Already a section of Manchester's ring road was named Alan Turing Way.

Then in 1999, his name appeared in *Time* magazine's list of the hundred most important people of the 20th century and *Princeton Alumni Weekly* named him the second most important alumnus after President James Madison, though he only came in at twenty-one in the 2002 BBC TV poll of the *100 Greatest Britons*.

A statue of Turing was unveiled at Bletchley Park in 2007. There is another in Manchester which has an Amstrad – one of the most popular early home computers in the UK – buried under its plinth.

In 2011, Turing's papers were put up for auction. IT journalist Gareth Halfacree raised £28,500 by public subscription, Google followed with another $100,000 and Britain's National Heritage Memorial Fund stepped in with £213,437. This allowed the papers to be purchased and kept at Bletchley Park.

Turing's contribution to intellectual life has been commemorated in universities around the world. Statues have been erected and buildings and prizes have been named after him.

In November 2011 the life of Alan Turing came to the TV screen again with Channel Four's *Britain's Greatest Codebreaker*. This featured dramatizations of conversations that were supposed to have taken place between Turing and Franz Greenbaum and assumed that Turing did take his own life. In a follow-up article entitled 'Turing Committed Suicide: Case Closed', the producers Patrick Sammon and Paul Sen maintained that Greenbaum thought that 'suicide was the most likely scenario'. They also pointed out that four months before he died 41-year-old Turing had made a will, taking this as 'evidence of premed-itation'. But biographer Andrew Hodges pointed out that in his will

The statue of Alan Turing in Manchester's Sackville Park was unveiled on 23 June – Turing's birthday – in 2001

he had made provision for his housekeeper, Mrs Clayton, saying she 'should have a further £10 for each year in which she had been employed after the end of 1953 – a strange point to add if he had then been settled on death'.

Apple's famous once-bitten apple logo is erroneously said to be a tribute to Turing. When British writer-actor-presenter and all-round technophile Stephen Fry asked Apple's founder Steve Jobs if this was the case, Jobs said: 'God we wish it were. It's just a coincidence.'

To mark the centenary of his birth, 2012 was declared 'Alan Turing Year', with events being staged in over fifty countries. Britain issued a commemorative postage stamp.

ROYAL PARDON

After a petition in 2009 attracted over 30,000 signatures, British Prime Minister Gordon Brown issued an official apology over Turing's treatment, saying: 'Without his outstanding contribution, the history of the Second World War could well have been very different.'

In December 2011, another petition was raised asking for a posthumous pardon. This was at first opposed by the government, but when a bill granting Turing a statutory pardon was introduced in the House of Lords, the government changed its mind. On 24 December 2013, the Queen signed a pardon under the little-known Royal Prerogative of Mercy. Immediately gay rights campaigner Peter Tatchell called for an enquiry into Turing's death 'if only to dispel any doubts about the true cause of death, including speculation that he was murdered by the security services'.

Turing's wartime achievements as a codebreaker have now been celebrated in the movie *The Imitation Game*, starring Benedict Cumberbatch as Turing. According to colleague Donald Michie, Turing's legacy lives on, not just in books, plays and films, but all around us:

'Alan Turing is one of the figures of the century. His consequences are everywhere and nobody knows now where it's going to take us. The world of computing and now the world of the internet stems from Alan Turing's fundamental ideas. There were other great men at Bletchley Park, but in the long, long wall of history I think Turing's name will probably be the number one in terms of consequences for mankind.'

Further Reading

Alan M. Turing by Sara Turing, Cambridge University Press, Cambridge, 2012

Alan Turing and His Contemporaries: Building the World's First Computers edited by Simon Lavington, British Informatics Society, Swindon, Wiltshire, 2012

Alan Turing: The Architect of the Computer Age by Ted Gottfried, Franklin Watts, New York, 1996

Alan Turing: The Enigma by Andrew Hodges, Simon and Schuster, New York, 1983

Codebreakers: The Inside Story of Bletchley Park edited by F.H. Hinsley and Alan Stripp, Oxford University Press, Oxford, 1993

The Essential Turing: Seminal Writings in Computing, Logic, Philosophy, Artificial Intelligence and Artificial Life, plus the Secrets of Enigma edited by B. Jack Copeland, Clarendon Press, Oxford, 2004

Makers of Modern Science: Alan Turing – Computing Genius and Wartime Code Breaker by Harry Henderson, Chelsea House, New York, 2011

Real Lives: Alan Turing – Codebreaker, Scientist, Genius, Lifesaver by Jim Eldridge, A&C Black, London, 2013

The Secret Life of Bletchley Park: The History of the Wartime Codebreaking Centre by the Men and Women Who Were There by Sinclair McKay, Aurum, London, 2010

Station X: The Codebreakers of Bletchley Park by Michael Smith, Pan Books, London, 2004

Turing: Pioneer of the Information Age by B. Jack Copeland, Oxford University Press, Oxford, 2012

Turing's Cathedral: The Origins of the Digital Universe by George Dyson, Allen Lane, London 2012

Index